Early Pra

In the first few chapters of *My Father's Shadow*, I was reminded of the Hemingway quote, "There is nothing to writing. All you do is sit at a typewriter and bleed." Hopper crafted his collection of memories into a captivating, interconnected narrative. You aren't just reading about him, you are experiencing his journey from inside his soul.
–Ed Abell, author of *My Father's Keep*

The very best writing connects us—to each other and to our humanity. *My Father's Shadow* does exactly that. With precision and grace, Hopper invites us into pivotal moments in his life and then quietly holds up a mirror to show us a bit of ourselves. This gorgeous collection strikes the perfect balance between the particular and the universal reminding us that we are not alone.
–Kim Suhr, Director of Red Oak Writing and author of *Nothing to Lose* and *Maybe I'll Learn*

An extraordinary life. Universal truths. Shared experiences. It's all in here. Beautifully written and deeply emotional stories about the confusing and often painful journey through life. At times the stories portray an ordinary man living an extraordinary life. Other times, an extraordinary man living an ordinary life. Both utterly fulfilling. These stories are unique to the teller but evoke experiences universal to readers.
–Jennifer Rupp, writing contemporary and historical romance as Jennifer Trethewey, the *Highlanders of Balforss* Series

Myles Hopper's memoir, *My Father's Shadow*, comes to the reader in fragments colored by the vagaries of memory, the unreliability of personal observation, and the delights of imagination. Hopper reminds us that what really happened is not as important as what we make of it, and what we make of it evolves with the years. His willingness as a storyteller to explore his own missteps and failings gives this book its complexity, its resonance. These stories and anecdotes are full of the desire to better understand what makes Hopper and us, his readers, who we all are. These chapters are filled, too, with the ache, wonder, resolve, and love afforded by a long-lived and deeply interrogated life.

–Patricia Ann McNair, author of *And These Are the Good Times* and *The Temple of Air*

Throughout *My Father's Shadow*, Myles Hopper has written compelling, poignant stories about his family, himself, and the fascinating people he has encountered. He has an ability to write simply and clearly as he recounts complex memories and interpretations of events from his childhood to an advanced age. This collection reveals a deep understanding of human interactions and emotions, and it is easy yet powerful to envision parts of one's own life while reading what he so richly shares about his own.

–Maurice A. Sterns, Ph.D., Manager of Executive Development Program at The World Bank; Regional Director of Latin America Scholarship Program at Harvard University; editor of *Perspectives on Newfoundland Society and Culture*

For Jennifer,
Thank you for playing
such an important
role in the production
of this book! I've
learned a great
deal from your
own writing...
Myles

My Father's Shadow

MYLES HOPPER

Myles Hopper

Ten|16
PRESS

www.TEN16press.com - Waukesha, WI

For information, please contact:

Ten|16
PRESS
www.TEN16press.com
Waukesha, WI

Cover design by Kaeley Dunteman

An earlier version of "Exodus Redux" appeared in *Family Stories From the Attic*, Hidden Timber Books, 2017

An earlier version of "But One Mournful Chord" appeared in *The Jewish Literary Journal*, February 2017

A version of "And Then There Were Three" appears in *Friends: Voices on the Gift of Companionship*, 2020

For Catherine

*and for our children and children-in-law,
Michael and Regina, and Caroline and Taif*

TABLE OF CONTENTS

PREFACE

My Father's Shadow is a collection of personal narratives, nonfiction explorations of events that span a lifetime—from very early childhood to the present day, what some would consider "old age." A little boy burdened with hair the color red, his scarlet letter. A man late in life confronted with looming mortality. These are the bookends of a collection of personal narratives that aren't merely about myself—they are more universal than that. Some are joyous, such as fatherhood, finding one's "own skin," and remembrances of dear friends and family; others can be painful and distressing, such as childhood trauma, financial distress, racial and religious prejudice, even death and dying. *My Father's Shadow* delves deep into the pain and joy of growing—of life itself.

Parts of stories that are told in early pages make additional appearances throughout the rest of the book. Characters and events move back and forth in time, the same way our memories present themselves in unexpected flashbacks and associations—the way so many of us remember our lives. My own process of remembering was often like standing in an editing studio ankle-deep in old-fashioned, raw film footage, searching for missing pieces. Some were found and memories were refreshed; others, alas, are lost for what could be forever.

It has taken a long time for this book to appear. The first draft of one of the stories in this book was written in 1992, then languished in a file folder for the next twenty-six years. Before it had been relegated to that folder, another author had encouraged me to finish it, and then the rest of the stories I wanted to tell. I told him I probably wouldn't—actually, I told him I couldn't—though writing was what I most wanted to do. To his "Why?" I said, "Because, I don't know if I'm able to tell the truth, and if I don't, none of this is worth writing about."

"The truth about what?"

"About my relationships with members of my family, my father, most of all. There was a great deal of love and caring, but there also was violence and rage, and I still have trouble dealing with the lifelong aftermath."

"Then I guess you have a decision to make."

Several years ago, I did make the decision to finish what I had begun. It helped to keep in mind Joan Didion's final sentence in "The Preface" to *Slouching Towards Bethlehem*. Reflecting upon how her interests as a writer might run counter to the interests of those she writes about, she concluded: "That is one last thing to remember: *writers are always selling somebody out*." [emphasis hers]

My goal has been to provide readers an opportunity similar to the one I have had in writing this book: to gain new perspectives on some of their own life experiences, to discover something of value that might have eluded them, and to gain a deeper understanding of themselves. The stories in the first part of this book acknowledge childhood trauma, tragic losses, and confusing, sometimes violent relationships within a family. But, they also celebrate the love and reconciliation that can prevail when any one of us finds a way to release the burden of debilitating memories and feelings that had become central to a sense of self. Taken as a whole, the stories demonstrate that for so many of us confusion and self-doubt, grief, fear, even depression are inevitable, but moving beyond them is possible, no matter how difficult it might be, no matter how long it might take. The result can be transcendent: rejection, anger, and blame can be balanced by love, acceptance, and forgiveness.

Recently, I was walking to an appointment and turned onto a paved path between two office buildings. I stopped in my tracks when I saw the path was strewn with wet and shiny golden leaves fallen from a line of honey locust trees. The scene reminded me of Gerard Manley Hopkins' "Spring and Fall: to a young child," a poem familiar to so many of us, and one that I memorized more than fifty years ago. It has been in my thoughts each day that I write. The poem captures what I had begun to feel in early childhood and would continue to feel as the heart grew older, and grows older yet. I remained on the path and recited, in a whisper:

Márgarét, áre you gríeving
Over Goldengrove unleaving?
Leáves like the things of man, you
With your fresh thoughts care for, can you?
Áh! ás the heart grows older
It will come to such sights colder
By and by, nor spare a sigh
Though worlds of wanwood leafmeal lie;
And yet you wíll weep and know why.

Now no matter, child, the name:
Sórrow's spríngs áre the same.
Nor mouth had, no nor mind, expressed
What heart heard of, ghost guessed:
It ís the blight man was born for,
It is Margaret you mourn for.

Rather than feeling bound by weeping, sorrow, and mourning, I fantasized that the path had been strewn with golden coins from an overflowing chest—an unexpected bounty. This was one more powerful moment when I was reminded that the feelings of abundance and well-being had long since occupied most of the space where feelings of scarcity, disappointment, and abandonment had dwelled within me. For this reason, it was especially gratifying when an early reader of several stories said, "How you handled what you went through gives me hope that I can get to the point you're at now." We agreed that resilience is what matters most.

If nothing else, the stories in *My Father's Shadow* reveal much about how one person has been able to love and be loved, and to thrive in a world replete with wild imperfections and an eclectic array of people and relationships, some nurturing, others much less so.

~ ~ ~ ~

All of us know, but too often forget, that our memories are influenced by many things, not the least of which is the passage of time. I was reminded of this recently while reading Umberto Eco's *The Name of the Rose*. The now-elderly narrator,

Adso, tells of a conversation he had when he was a young
Benedictine novice:

> Salvatore did not tell me only this tale. In broken
> words . . . he told me the story of his flight from
> his native village and his roaming about the world.
> And in his story I recognized many men I had
> already known or encountered along the road, and
> I now recognize many more that I have met since,
> so that after all this time I may even attribute to
> him adventures and crimes that belonged to others,
> before him and after him, and which now, in my
> tired mind, flatten out to form a single image.
> This, in fact, is the power of the imagination,
> which, combining the memory of gold with that
> of the mountain, can compose the idea of a golden
> mountain.

We can be certain that among all of the people, including
me, who appear in *My Father's Shadow*, there will be conflated
and conflicting memories and interpretations of events that
are irreconcilable. It's inevitable that this will happen to some
degree in almost anything written in the broad genre of
memoir. What George Eliot wrote in *Middlemarch* is but one
additional way of reminding us of this inevitability:

"The memory has as many moods as the temper, and shifts
its scenery like a diorama."

Shorewood, Wisconsin, 2020

PART I

The Color Red

All children's parents are too complicated for them. Certainly my father was too complicated for me. Love, like an obstacle, gets in the way. We know them too early. Then they die.
—Stanley Elkin, "My Father's Life"

THE COLOR RED

A Crosswalk, Circa 1948

On the way to his maternal grandparents' apartment, the five-year-old boy in the back seat is just big enough to see out of his side window and watch the fall leaves floating downward. His father stops the car at a crosswalk to let an old woman cross in front of the car. Captivated, the boy hooks his fingers on the doorframe of his open window and pulls himself up so he can watch her short, deliberate steps toward the sidewalk on his side.

She wears high, laced, black shoes and a tan cardigan sweater, buttoned against the chilly autumn air. So bent forward is she by the weight of the shopping bags in each hand— her arms extended to their fullest, her shoulders hunched and rounded—that she could not possibly see anything but the asphalt at her feet.

His hands still on the doorframe, he leans farther out the open window and looks back at the woman as his father slowly drives away. The boy wonders why his mother and father in the front seat, and his brother next to him, don't seem to pay any attention to the disturbing sight.

And where are the children of the old lady?

As he has done during the many Sabbath and holiday

dinners at his grandparents' apartment, on this early evening the boy sits with three generations and extensions that comprise this family: his father and mother, his brothers, aunts, uncles, cousins, and sometimes sisters and cousins of his grandmother and grandfather, addressed as "Mom" and "Pop" by their three children.

At the familiar table, the boy is visited by the same intense sadness he felt as he watched the old woman in the crosswalk an hour earlier. How sad Mom and Pop must be, he thinks; how unhappy they must be that they don't have children of their own, and must live alone. He concludes on this Sabbath that regular visits to the old people are to offer reprieve from their loneliness and abandonment.

Though he does not know it yet, each passing year will bring a deeper understanding of why he was so disturbed at the crosswalk and confused at his grandparents' table. He will understand that he carried in each hand his own heavy bags as he stepped through a different kind of crosswalk, often feeling abandoned, frightened he might not reach the other side.

Los Angeles, 1988

The distressed voices of a woman and child reached me from the alcove of pay phones in the lobby of the Holiday Inn near the airport. The woman held a telephone receiver to her ear. A five- or six-year-old boy cried while leaning against his mother's leg. He wore a T-shirt and wide-legged shorts that made his thin legs seem vulnerable. His shorts, even the T-shirt were like mine when I was his age.

The mother used her free hand to hug her boy against her leg.

"I told you," she said into the phone, exasperated. "I couldn't find it in my bag when we tried to check in . . . what? I don't believe this."

"Mommy, don't cry," the boy said.

She placed the receiver ever so slowly into its cradle.

"Excuse me," I said to her, "but do you need help?"

She said yes, and explained that their flight was from Sydney to Toronto, with a layover in L.A. until that night. Qantas had provided her with a Holiday Inn coupon, which she now couldn't find. Over the phone, Qantas had told her to go back to the airport for a replacement, but she and her little boy were too exhausted, and the hotel manager said he wouldn't help her unless she could "produce" a coupon.

With that, she covered her forehead with the palm of her hand and appeared to be at the end of her ability to cope. For a moment, that boy was the boy I had been forty years earlier watching the old lady in the crosswalk. Now, I could feel his loneliness, his fear, in what could have been his own crosswalk disguised as a cheap lobby in a Holiday Inn. I didn't want to abandon him and his mother, so I asked if I might talk to the manager on their behalf. She said she'd appreciate it, and took the few steps to the nearest couch. She slumped against the back cushion and closed her eyes as her boy rested his head against her.

"Yes? May I assist you?" the front desk manager said through a tight smile confined to the corners of his mouth.

"You know about the woman and little boy? From Qantas?"

"Of course. What would you like me to do, sir?" Another tight smile.

"For one thing, stop being so passive-aggressive. Then, give them a room."

He told me that even if he could give them a room, he didn't have any, and I used what remained of my self-control to inform him that he did have a room: I had decided to leave a day early; they could take my room.

"I'll pay for the extra day," I said to give him no plausible reason to refuse. "You'll have the room made up for them right away, correct? I'll leave my bag here until late this afternoon."

He scribbled a note of some kind on his memo pad. "Why are you doing this?"

"Because I am," I told him. "Don't take any money from her. And don't tell her I paid. Just tell her you decided to help her and her boy."

I returned to the couch where mother and child sat in repose. "They're getting your room ready now."

"I can't possibly thank you enough," she said, exhaling with relief as her boy slept, his cheek against her shoulder. She asked for my business card, which I handed her and said goodbye.

A week later, I received a "thank-you" letter, but decided there was no need to reply. Had her little redheaded boy written a note or drawn a picture of a kangaroo, a koala bear, or an airplane—maybe all of them together—I think I would have answered.

A Question, Circa 1948

Only months after watching the old lady in the crosswalk, the little boy holds his mother's hand as they climb the flight of front hall steps to his grandparents' apartment. For the first time, he asks his mother a question that has troubled him for as long as he can remember. "I don't like my red hair," he says. "When I'm big will it be dark?" He half hopes she will say no and tell him how lucky he is to have red hair, how handsome it is, how much she loves it.

But she doesn't say this. Instead, she says, "Yes, it will. When you're older, your hair will be dark."

So that is it. His mother has confirmed his suspicion that his hair color is something to wish away.

"When you're older, your hair will be dark," she repeats with a slight smile and tilt of her head.

In his despair, he hopes she is telling the truth, that the red hair won't be with him forever. But she is not. The color red will follow him through the years and decades to come, his own scarlet letter.

Revelation Day, 1968

I was in my mid-twenties when my father called and asked if I had time to come to his and my mother's apartment. I lived nearby, so it took only fifteen minutes to drop what I was doing and get there.

"We have something important to tell you," he said. He and my mother settled into the couch, while I sat on the edge of the seat of a matching chair. Without further preamble, he said, "I was adopted, by Saul and Minnie Hopper."

He used their family name, as if I wouldn't realize he was talking about my deceased grandparents.

"I've known for years, but I still don't know who my real mother and father are." Perhaps in response to how incredulous I looked, he added, "Maybe we should have told you earlier."

"Maybe?" The chair bobbed under me, a boat rolling on swells caused by some faraway storm. Nothing under me felt solid, nothing was stable.

My mother continued the story. "When your father proposed to me, he said, 'Sylvia, I know I'm not good enough for you.' I said, 'Because you're adopted? That doesn't matter to me at all,' and your father said, 'What are you talking about?'" She paused. "I've never forgotten how deeply it hurt him to find out in this way."

Until that moment, I was absorbed in my own feelings about this revelation and not how my father might have felt. "I hope you're okay, Dad," I said.

"I am," he said with a slight, reassuring nod. "I am. When I told my parents that I'd learned I was adopted, they said all they knew was my biological parents were good people . . . 'not a prostitute, not a reprobate' is how they put it." His eyes watered.

"I wish you would've told me all this years ago."

"We probably should have," my mother said.

Dismayed by the *maybe* and the *probably* and the fact that they'd kept this secret from their children for all of these years, I asked whether my two brothers knew. Apparently, they had been told a day earlier.

As preoccupied as I was with what I'd just learned, I almost didn't ask how my mother had known about the adoption. When I did, she made the cryptic comment that along with the adoptive parents, "A few people knew." My parents and I must have wanted to avoid going any deeper into this topic; because I didn't ask who they were, and she didn't volunteer, it wasn't until many years later that I would learn their identities.

Revelation Day II, 1984

My wife, Catherine, and I had been living in St. Louis for the past three years. The phone rang as I was just about to leave for the airport to pick her up after her visit to her extended family in Wisconsin.

It was my younger brother calling.

"I'm with Mom and Dad," he said. He sounded calm, but concerned, as he explained that they had asked him and his wife to come to their condominium, and they wanted Catherine and me to be there, also.

I was frustrated by the unexpected and untimely request, and said I had to pick up Catherine at the airport. My brother was insistent. He said that his wife would go to the airport for Catherine, and it would be a good idea for me to join him and my parents. Now. No longer frustrated, I worried that some terrible news awaited.

Ten minutes later, I was listening to my parents continue the story of my father's adoption, the story they had begun sixteen years earlier, in 1968.

My mother spoke first. "You remember we said we didn't know who your father's biological parents were?" She and my father had been reclining against the cushions of the couch, but now she leaned forward. "Well, that's no longer the truth."

"Wait, Mom." I was afraid she was about to tell a story the way she sometimes did, packed with references to people I couldn't remember or never knew, and other names and facts, all of which could be mystifying and sometimes infuriating. I wouldn't let this be one of those times. Because she is the same mother who once said to me that if I speak with my younger brother, I should tell him that if he speaks with our older brother, to ask him to call her, I said, "I really need you to be clear, Mom. Do you mean you *did* know in 1968, or it's only *now* that you know?"

"Only now. Well, recently," she said.

I wanted to ask what she meant by "recently," but I waited.

My father leaned forward on the couch. "Mark and Rose, my grandparents, had eight children, and my father, Saul, was one of them."

"You mean your *adoptive* father, Saul, right?"

"Right. He married Minnie, so that's how she became my adoptive mother. Saul had a younger sister, Sadie, who was twenty-one when she gave birth to a son . . . me. But she wasn't married. She gave me to her brother, Saul, and his wife, Minnie, who were childless, and they raised me as their own child."

My breathing became shallow. I was on the boat again, bobbing on ocean swells. Nothing felt stable beneath me, nothing solid. "Aunt Sadie"—the aunt he had told me about years ago, the one who took him on outings—was his mother . . . or *one* of his mothers?

"Minnie was such a wonderful mother to me." He was fighting back the tears. "I just can't express how much she helped me."

"Well, who was the . . . your biological father?"

"His name was Max, and he was Sadie's uncle."

"Sadie's *uncle*? Her *uncle*?"

"By marriage," my mother said in a matter-of-fact way that surprised me, given how unusual the information was. "He'd married a sister of Sadie's mother."

"This is hard to absorb, but I'm sure trying," I said to her.

I turned back to my father. "All I ever knew was that you told me how much you loved being with your Aunt Sadie."

"She was young, and a lot of fun, and she took me in a little red convertible on outings around the city. After a while, I began to feel guilty."

"What about, Dad?"

He paused to collect himself. "I loved Sadie and wanted her to be my mother. But Minnie was my mother, and I loved her, too." He paused again. "I was just a little boy."

"Dad, I understand." I knew how hard this conversation was for my father, but also how liberating it must be. My eyes filled with tears. At that moment, he and I both were once again just little boys. "But, honestly, this is nothing you have to feel guilty about."

I turned to my mother. "How'd you find out about all of this, Mom? And when?"

She told me it was when she and my father had visited Catherine and me in New Hampshire. We'd driven down to Boston to have dinner with my father's cousin, Joe, and his wife, Dorothy. On our way into the restaurant, my mother and Dorothy stayed a few steps behind us. She said to Dorothy that even though my father was adopted, he sure looked like all the other Hoppers. That's when Dorothy said, "That's because he *is* a Hopper."

Before my mother could continue, I said, "And you just stopped talking and ate dinner?"

"No. Dorothy and I agreed to talk privately after dinner. Later, at their house, she told me that she and Joe and other family members had known the whole story all along."

My mother revealed this information in a calm voice, never saying she was surprised, or shocked, or even relieved to have learned the truth, finally.

"But that was 1979, Mom. You didn't tell Dad for five years? Until today?"

"Yesterday," my mother continued, "your brother insisted I tell your father immediately, so I did this afternoon. Right after that, your brother came here."

"Mom asked me to be here for moral support," he said. "I'm glad you were able to come over here right away."

She had told both of my brothers during the previous week, after our father had begun asking what she knew about his adoption. Afraid she would hurt him again, as she had when he proposed, she put off completing the story until she just couldn't hold it from him any longer.

Up to this point in the conversation, my father had sat deep in the corner of the couch, looking smaller than he was, as if taking up less space could protect him from being overwhelmed by his memories and emotions while listening to the revelation for the second time in one day. Now, he sat more upright, even smiled a little. I don't know what he was feeling at that moment, but I assumed he felt relieved now that he had learned the truth.

Right then, Catherine arrived with my brother's wife and took the chair next to me. I took her hand, knowing that her presence would give me the emotional support that no one else in the room could. She had been briefed on the ride from the airport, so it wasn't necessary to repeat everything that had been said to me.

My mother continued the story.

"When your dad neared thirteen, Max was the one who helped him study for his bar mitzvah."

My father added, "When your mother told me about Sadie and Max, I finally knew that what Saul and Minnie had said about my biological mother and father not being *lowlifes* or *reprobates* was really true."

Even though Max was, in fact, a reprobate, my parents seemed willing to compartmentalize that reality. After all, he was my father's father—or *one* of them. I ached when I imagined the two of them in the intimate moments of a father helping his son become a man through the ritual of our religion. I wanted to know, but didn't ask, where was his adoptive father, Saul, during these sessions? Did he watch and listen? Did he want to be his son's teacher and guide? What remarkable and selfless people Saul and Minnie must have been.

Then, my parents reminded me of another bittersweet issue within this entire drama.

Sometime prior to my father's eleventh birthday, Sadie married a man named Lou. She died a very short time after giving birth to their daughter, Deborah. Lou, having become a single father, followed what had been established as acceptable family behavior: until he might be able to assume the responsibilities of child-rearing, he gave the infant to Saul and Minnie.

Several years later, Lou remarried and took back
Deborah. He said it would be best for the two families not
to visit because it would be too difficult for all concerned.
My father and Deborah had become very close, loved each
other, and grieved their entire lives over the separation. My
father always had referred to her as his "little sister," even
though he'd believed, until Revelation Day II, that she was
his cousin.

"This is just absolutely astonishing," I said. "So, now
all of us should meet with Debbie and her children, right?
We've been with her and her family many times, but none of
us . . . except you, Mom . . . knew the truth. Debbie needs
to know the truth, and her children need to know they have
some cousins they thought were just friends of the family."

"We'll call and see when we can visit," my mother said.

As I had failed to do during Revelation Day I, when
I hadn't asked my mother who had told her about the
adoption, I didn't say during Revelation Day II, "Hold on
a minute, Mom. Why did you prod Dorothy the way you
did? You must have thought you already knew, right? Or
even *knew* you knew." As I tried to make sense of all this
new information and my intense and conflicting feelings,
my mother handed me a photograph in a simple, black
wooden frame.

"This is your grandmother, Sadie, and her mother,
Rose—your great-grandmother. It likely was taken around
the time Sadie gave birth to your father in 1914."

The two women stood side by side, wearing similar,
high-collared dresses adorned with intricate lace. Sadie's
left hand rested on Rose's right shoulder. Neither mother

nor daughter was smiling. I recognized them from other photographs, and always had known that Sadie and I resembled each other. But now, I was even more aware of what we shared: the shape of our chins, our long noses, our dark eyes, like those of her mother.

"You couldn't have known this from any of the black-and-white photographs in our albums," my mother said, "but your grandmother, Sadie, was a redhead."

"She was *what*? A redhead?"

My mother looked at me sideways with a tilt of her head, wearing her I-understand-how-you-feel look. I stifled my urge to express my utter dismay and anger, and somehow kept from saying, "Do you and Dad even come close to understanding how I feel at this moment? Do you even come close to understanding how unhappy, even ashamed, I've been to be a redhead? I'm that little boy who wanted his red hair to be dark, and you told him it would be. And, Dad, of course you remember your rage and how many times it turned to violence for reasons I only now begin to understand."

I became aware that for the past few moments, I had been touching the thin, white scar on my upper lip, just below the nose, as I sometimes do.

A Photograph, Circa 1951

The boy smiles at the camera as if there's nothing unusual about the dark scab that begins at the bottom of his nose and extends to just above the upper lip that struck the edge of the Formica and aluminum kitchen table. There is no record of an urgent trip to the home of a doctor who treats the wound. The boy asks himself what he did that was so terribly wrong to deserve this punishment from his father.

Later, when the photograph is taken, the boy still asks himself what he did wrong. Even today, even knowing better, he still wonders.

I looked up from the photograph I'd been holding and said nothing about my disturbing memory. Instead, I said to my father, "Sadie . . . one of my grandmothers. She's really pretty, Dad. I'm really happy my red hair comes from someone you loved." I'd never seen him look so vulnerable yet so comfortable letting those around him know it. He smiled at me, and again his tears were obvious.

For a reason I couldn't identify, I found it difficult to accept that long before Revelation Day II he hadn't known or at least thought—not just wished—that redheaded Sadie, who had taken him on outings, the one he wanted to be his mother, in fact had given birth to him.

I refrained from asking the barrage of questions racing through my mind: Did my father share my belief that when he'd hurt me, when his anger had crossed the invisible line to violence, it had been because my hair reminded everyone of Sadie and the "shame" of my father's "illegitimacy"? Were there other reasons that I, the middle of his three sons, had been the one to bear the brunt of his anger? These were considerations so complex that none of us ever fully understood the reasons for his difficulty in controlling his anger and aggression, waiting below the surface until something caused it to erupt at unexpected moments.

One year later, almost to the day, my father died. Not once had we spoken to each other about Sadie's and my hair and its significance in our relationship, especially during my childhood, but also for decades beyond.

He had wished that Sadie would be his mother. And from the moment I learned the truth about his birth, I wished he would have said, just once, how lucky I was to have red hair, and how handsome it was. I wished he would have said, "When I think about how much I loved Sadie and her red hair, I think about *your* hair and how much I've always loved it—and you, too. I know I hurt you, in part because of it. And I hope you've forgiven me."

But, he didn't say it.

My Mother's Death, 1999

During the years after my father died, the few times my mother and I talked about my childhood and the significance of my red hair, neither of us had been comfortable having these conversations. I'd been careful not to explode, and she'd been careful to avoid saying anything she thought might provoke me. And I needed to be just as careful not to provoke her.

She must have understood I was dancing around the edges of "I can't remember your ever trying to stop Dad when he was in a rage, but did you? Did you say anything when the two of you were alone? Who came to get me when I fled through the kitchen, past the table, and out the screen door with the hook and eye latch? Did you scream to heaven when your little boy couldn't run fast enough to escape the painful sting on his back from one swipe of a metal coat hanger that his thin T-shirt couldn't block? Do you know how many years it took for me to understand I had done nothing wrong, nothing bad enough to deserve this?"

A Mother's Remark, Circa 1958

"When you were born, you were covered in reddish fuzz that was wet and matted."

The boy is a teenager when his mother tells him this, and he will never forget it. She wears the same face she might wear for sour food and bad news. The redness of the fuzz, the redness of his hair, his mother's expression, all meld together. That she found it ugly hurts the boy. That she couldn't stop herself from saying it hurts him even more.

A few years before my mother died, she came the closest to acknowledging that she understood why I had felt hurt, even abandoned, by her. In what had to have been for her a moment of confession, and was for me a moment of confirmation, she told me, "When you were born, your grandfather said, 'Wasn't one child enough?'" She gave one of her wan smiles and a tilt of her head.

I was dumbfounded. Neither my mother nor I said aloud what I imagined both of us were thinking: My older brother, her firstborn, was blond; her father thought she should have quit while she and the entire extended family were ahead. It was painful for me to link my grandfather's words to those of my mother, years earlier, about my wet and matted hair at birth.

The words of my grandfather shaped my pain, yet it was through the words of my mother that the pain was inflicted. It might be the pain associated with the memory that, even now, causes me to wonder: Did she mean her own father had spoken those words, or did she mean it was her father-in-law? For as long as I can remember, I have believed the words were her father's. Years later, I would uncover something, a letter, that would make it more difficult for me to believe the words had been spoken by someone else.

Feeling empty, all I could manage was, "Because I had red hair."

"I don't know . . ."

Before she could finish the thought, I said, "Well, I do. For God's sake, Mom, what an absolutely outrageous thing to say. He was talking about my hair, and you knew why."

I couldn't determine whether I was angrier at my

grandfather or at her. First, it was *your hair will be dark when you're older*; then, *your red hair was wet and matted when you were born*; then, *wasn't one child enough?* The combination of dissembling, the lack of impulse control, and the retentive way she withheld information only to reveal it piece by piece was confusing and hurtful, as it always had been. She might have had more to say, but didn't say it. She might have understood better than I did, that I was unable to listen, that all I would be able to do was blame her.

I never did stop dancing around the edges of the honest conversation we needed to have before my mother died.

On the Patio, Midsummer 2016

Sitting at the patio table looking at a group of photos from my childhood, Catherine and I had nothing to do but enjoy the warm sun and cool breeze from nearby Lake Michigan. I might have left it that way, but didn't.

"Do you remember my father wanted only one song to be sung during his funeral service: 'Sometimes I Feel Like a Motherless Child'?"

"And do *you* remember he told me that he wanted something different than the traditional Jewish funeral ceremony?" Catherine said.

"You mean just in case the spiritual coming right after the rabbi and mourners said the holy *Kaddish* wouldn't have been different enough?"

Ignoring my attempt at humor, she reminded me that he told her he wanted a New Orleans jazz band. He liked telling Catherine these sorts of things when she would pick him up at the auto repair shop, or when they'd talk after she had run an errand for him. He loved her.

"Right after your father died, I mentioned to your mother what he had told me about the New Orleans jazz band, and she said, 'I know what Ed wanted, but I have to do it the way our family and our tradition do it.' He probably had told her about it more than once."

I'm sure my father's preference for his funeral ceremony had been sincere, and not one of his more provocative and maddening pronouncements: "This is the era of the bulldozer" or "A man has to love his family to barbecue in such heat." And many others. My mother's decision hadn't been wrong, I suppose, since funerals are for the quick, not the dead.

Oh, but how I would have loved to hear someone singing those forlorn words that had meant so much to my father: *Sometimes I feel like a motherless child . . . A long ways from home.* How I would have enjoyed celebrating my father's life by stepping to the beat of New Orleans jazz straight through the wide-open double doors of the Jewish funeral parlor and into the wide-open rear door of the hearse. In my imagination, the rabbi would grip his prayer book tight against his chest while leaning into a windstorm of holy retribution, worthy of the worst that God had to offer. His other hand would anchor his *yarmulke* so it wouldn't fly from his head, all the while lifting his eyes heavenward: "It's not *my* fault. I didn't think he actually *meant* it." Oh, but how I would have enjoyed that funeral!

On the patio, Catherine and I finished our coffee. She went inside, and I sat alone, marveling at the many colors and textures of the flower garden. I considered a grouping of three prolific, red rosebushes and remembered the father who had turned small plots of infertile ground by the side of our apartment building into beautiful rose gardens. When I was a teenager, and later as an adult, I hadn't offered to help tend them. My unwillingness to help angered him.

It was difficult to understand why my father so often

asked for help in ways that felt more like a demand than an invitation. There were times when I wanted to participate, but even when he invited me in an inclusive manner, I didn't know how to accept. What to him might have seemed like a "simple invitation" was never simple, either in the offering or in the acceptance or refusal, even with a good excuse.

In truth, I always was concerned that working with him might create the expectation that I was willing to become his co-gardener. What, then, would his response be if the next time I were to refuse? Underlying all of our confusing lack of clear communication was another question: Were we, in fact, avoiding the discomfort of intimacy?

We had a hard time with this, he and I. Not always. But often.

I had a sudden impulse to walk to the garage and take in my masterpiece of cleanliness and order. I began my pleasurable séance. *Father, behold this garage. Tools and supplies and implements hanging on the walls and stored on shelves. Shovels and lumber stored on decking on the rafters. I see you are pleased, Father.*

My feelings of closeness to my father were tempered by the intrusive thought of what might have been his reaction had he seen the garage before I had cleaned and organized it after a period of neglect that garages seem to insist upon.

His frequent expressions of disapproval—sometimes nothing more than a devastating shaking of the head and a turning away—were so different from the scoutmaster-father, the baseball coach-father, always nurturing, teaching, mentoring, parenting in such a magnificent way. I stood at the doorway and wondered how it could be that I was still trying to please him when I was seventy-three and a father of two. It took but a few seconds of wondering before I recalled the Isaac Asimov clipping from New York Times I had saved in my desk drawer:

> In *In Memory Yet Green*, the first volume of his autobiography, published in 1979, he explained how he became a compulsive writer. His Russian-born father owned a succession of candy stores in Brooklyn that were open from 6 A.M. to 1 A.M. seven days a week. Young Isaac got up at 6 o'clock every morning to deliver papers and rushed home from school to help out in the store every afternoon. If he was even a few minutes late, his father yelled at him for being a *folyack*, Yiddish for sluggard. Even more than 50 years later, he wrote: "It is a point of pride with me that though I have an alarm clock, I never set it, but get up at 6 A.M. anyway. I am still showing my father I'm not a *folyack*.

Catherine returned to the patio with a fresh pot of coffee and invited our neighbor, Frank, to join us. Soon, the three of us were talking about our families and looking at the photos I had brought outside.

"You're focused on that one more than the others," Frank said, nodding at a photo I held in my hand.

"I've looked at this dozens of times." I passed it to him. "That's my father's shadow. He's taking the picture, and you see it must be late afternoon. He's using one of those old box cameras with the pop-up viewfinder you had to hold at your waist so you could see what you're shooting. That's why his hands aren't part of the shadow."

"What a great photo," Frank said.

"I don't feel so great about it, Frank," I said.

After he chided me for failing to "honor thy father," Catherine said, "You look like such a sweet young boy lying on the grass, propped up on your elbows with your chin resting in your hands. It's lovely."

"Thanks for saying that, sweetheart, but I think I look like an irritated seven- or eight-year-old who doesn't want to pose for a picture. What bothers me, though, is the shadow. It looks like it's about to cover me. Like that movie what's-its-name with the shadow of the alien mother ship—can you say "father ship"?—moving across the ground before you even see what that colossal spacecraft looks like."

"*Independence Day,*" Frank said. "But, you're wrong. Your dad wants to take your picture, and that's all there is to it."

"And I don't want him to, and I'm pissed off."

"You do look annoyed," Catherine said, "but I think it might be one of those times when you look annoyed, but you're really pleased."

"Could be you're both right. You're not, but that's okay."

A Train Station, Fall 1945

The small boy is two and a half years old. He's waiting in a crowded train station with his older brother and his mother. The boy's G.I. father is coming home. World War II is over.

Tired from the waiting and uncomfortable with all the commotion, the boy bursts into tears when his mother hands him to his father, a stranger he hasn't seen for a good portion of his young life. Though it will become emblematic, at least for the boy, they will never speak of this significant event in their history as father and son.

Forty years after the incident, the boy will retell the story to his friend, who asks, "During all these years, did you ever consider how your father must have felt?"

The boy's answer?

A disconcerting and embarrassed, "No."

Frank, Catherine, and I drank some more coffee and just enjoyed each other's company. After a while, he left, Catherine went inside, and I sat alone trying to understand how I felt. More than thirty years had gone by since Revelation Day II when I had learned the truth about my father and redheaded Sadie . . . about myself . . . who I was and where I'd come from. Yet, the sanguine feeling that came from knowing the full story, the truth, was intruded upon by a feeling of unease that I tried to ignore.

I placed the photo on the stack I had brought outside, secured it with the rubber band, and did what I had done hundreds, even thousands of times—I walked into the largest flower bed still bathed in the lovely, late afternoon sunlight, and immediately felt safe within it, embraced by the midsummer bloom. The intense and welcome fragrance of sweet alyssum pervaded the patio, but didn't mask the apple-sweet fragrance of the tall, white rosebush. I had often complained about mildew, black spot, and Japanese beetles, but hadn't resented taking care of our roses, no matter the memories of another rose garden— my father's. With a very light touch, I drew a fingertip across the needle-sharp point of a thick thorn on the bush.

A dangerous piece of work this thorn is . . . but, not always . . . it would hurt only if I press my finger too hard against it . . . but why would anyone . . . I . . . want to do that? How easy it would be to press just a little bit harder . . . upset the delicate balance between an almost pleasant tickle of the tip of a thorn and a wounded finger and a drop of red blood . . . is this the feeling so many young people have when they cut themselves . . . remembering a childhood often marked with confusion, not knowing what to expect or when to expect it . . . or what to do when it happens.

I lingered, rearranging pots and deadheading cosmos and geraniums, as the sun dropped well below the roofline of our house, and the garden was in shadow. In this moment of silent transition, no longer day and not yet night, everything seemed suspended, and memories of events, recent and more remote, had room to return.

A few months earlier, there had been a phone conversation with my younger brother. Still trying to resolve my sometimes jumbled feelings, I had begun to doubt that I had an accurate memory of even the most obvious and fundamental facts concerning both Revelation Days, the adoption, Sadie, and my own childhood.

"Let me ask you something. I need to make sure I'm not imagining everything. Did Sadie have red hair?"

"Yes, she did."

"But here's what's even more difficult. You were born four years after I was. You had red hair, just like mine. Do I remember correctly that you didn't experience what I did from Dad? I know our older brother didn't."

"You remember correctly."

"So, if red hair had something to do with his behavior, it must have been mine. I was the first, and I guess I remained the target. You might have been one, too, but it wasn't like what happened to me."

"That's the way I remember it, too. You bore the brunt of his anger."

But there also was the subsequent exchange of emails, again with my younger brother.

Me: Do you remember when we first were told that Dad was adopted?

Brother: I was twenty-one, I think. It must have been 1968. Dad told me in the living room after turning down the lights for dramatic emphasis, and showing me the letter his adoptive mother had left for him to read after her death.

Me: What letter? I didn't remember there was a letter. Dad's adoptive mom, Minnie, died in 1937, before he had proposed to Mom. Someone sat on the letter, I guess, until at least right after he proposed.

Brother: Right. He hadn't read the letter, but insiders in the Jewish community, at least in their synagogue, knew the whole story. That's how Mom knew before Dad did. Probably the head rabbi was involved in the adoption, and he was close to Mom's father.

I remembered that on Revelation Day I, my parents did refer to the letter, but hadn't shown it to me (assuming they still had it). They said it didn't reveal the identities of my father's biological parents but had been careful to state that they weren't "reprobates." My mother must have learned about the adoption from her father; my father learned it from my mother; my brothers and I learned it from both of them; then, that process recurred on Revelation Day II.

But if that's all there is to the story, then why, I wondered, was I having the sort of feeling you have when you know the name of something or someone, but can't remember what it is? And why was I uneasy that I might?

And then, I did.

The Bus Stop, Circa 1952

"So, where did he get his red hair?" It's odd, but people only ask this question to the boy's mother, never his father.

"Ed's mother had red hair." She says this with her characteristic slight tilt and nod of her head, and a bit of a smile—a wordless, "Believe me."

The boy has no reason to question his mother's answer. From early in his childhood, whenever anyone directs the question to him, he keeps the answer at the ready and parrots it. From the time he is nine until he can drive his own car, he takes city buses. Waiting at the bus stop, he is often asked by men, "So, young man, where did you get your red hair?" and by women, "Where did you get your lovely (sometimes sweet or nice) red hair?"

To be asked this question by strangers makes him feel vulnerable; these are the only times he feels that way when riding the buses. "My dad's mother had red hair," he answers and looks away. Sometimes, when he has enough nerve, he moves a step or two away from the stranger.

Later, after he has learned the truth, the boy will wonder, but never ask, why his mother had said such a thing. Did she think his father would not have heard her? What if the boy had innocently mentioned to him his "mother's" red hair?

I returned to my chair at the patio table and for a while tried to organize all of the information and determine what information belonged in which category: *I believe it, I don't believe it, I don't have a clue.* The entire adoption story told by my parents was replete with too many instances of denial and avoidance, too many failures to acknowledge "I knew" or "I thought I knew," too many inconsistencies that begged to be resolved.

On that midsummer day, my beliefs crystalized: For years prior to her meeting with Dorothy in Boston, my mother had known or, at the very least, *thought* she knew that Sadie was my father's biological mother. My father must have suspected it, even as a little boy with a little boy's wish and a little boy's guilt over wanting Sadie to be his mother. The venerated rabbi, referred to in my brother's email, would have known about Sadie, not merely about the adoption—family members would have told him everything. The rabbi was close with my mother's father, so he must have known, as well, about Sadie—and, I believe, would have told my mother about her and not merely about the adoption. My mother must have understood what her father had meant by, "Wasn't one child enough?"

If she hadn't understood it, could she have kept from asking why he would say something so outrageous? I believed she hadn't needed to ask; it was inconceivable to me that the first time she would have been able to understand what her father had meant would have been thirty-six years later during a trip to Boston.

Reading His Grandfather's Letter, Midsummer 2016

Among the many papers and photographs his mother has bequeathed him, the boy discovers a letter to her from her father, dated August 11, 1944, when the boy is eighteen months old. His mother, his older brother, and he are at Fort Benning, Georgia, visiting her soldier husband, the boy's father, before he is scheduled to ship out to Europe and World War II. The grandfather, the father of the boy's mother, has chosen to write:

> *We received two little pictures in today's letter
> where you say [the boy] is about to say, "no."
> Mama says that he doesn't look like us. Look at
> the picture! Well, I will close with love and kisses
> to you all. Kiss the kids.*
> *Dad and Mom*

The boy, in disbelief, reads this part of the letter several times. He looks at photographs of himself at that age and might be looking at the very picture his grandparents received. He believes those words were another way of saying what already had been said a year and a half earlier: "Wasn't one child enough?" Another way of saying the child is "The Other," not one of us, does not belong. He returns the letter to its envelope.

In that instant, he is once again five, six, maybe seven . . . he can't remember. The dog is his older brother's. She gives birth to six puppies. One dies, and the boy's parents soon give the other five away. They've been sent to live on a farm, they tell him. He cries so long that all he can do is lie in bed while his mother puts cold washcloths on his forehead. He cries so hard that he gasps for air and says over and over, "I want my puppies . . . Where are my puppies? . . . I want my puppies!" But they are gone. They don't belong with us.

Victims

It took twenty years from the time of my mother's death in 1999 for me to gain a fuller appreciation of how much her father's words must have hurt her. I also have gained a fuller appreciation that her misleading reassurance, "When you're older, your hair will be dark," and her hurtful observation, "You were covered in reddish fuzz that was wet and matted," might have been as layered and dense as some of her stories.

By telling me about these two incidents, was she, in her limited way, without explanation, saying she didn't know how to cope with the trauma my birth caused within the family? Was she saying there were many times when she had wanted to tell me that she understood my pain as well as her own?

I don't know and never will.

What I do know is that each of us was too well-defended against the other to be able to explore our often contentious relationship, and to be able to talk in-depth about some of those life events that caused each of us our own special sorrow. As a result, we never helped each other heal.

What I do know is that if I'm ever asked, as I had been about my father and me, "Did you ever consider how your mother must have felt?" my answer will be, "Yes."

I was not the only victim.

Gifts

A year before she dies, his mother gives the boy the photograph of Sadie and Rose in its simple, black frame, the one he had seen fifteen years earlier, during Revelation Day II.

His wife searches for a silver frame to match Sadie's and her mother's Edwardian clothing, and gives it to him as a gift. He secures the photograph in the new frame and places it on the small table in his office where he sees it many times, every day.

He says he feels grounded when he thinks of Sadie as his origin.

He says whenever he sees her he feels like he belongs, like there's no shame in how he has ever looked, no shame in having worn the color red.

He says the photograph is a treasure he'd run back into a burning house to save.

～ ～ ～ ～ ～

His Jewish mother lies on her deathbed in St. Mary's Hospital. In a private, intimate moment, she tells his wife something before it's too late. "Every day, I asked God to send me someone to watch over my son, and he sent you to me, and every day, I thank Him."

～ ～ ～ ～ ～

A priest inquires if he can pray with her. She says yes. "I appreciate all prayer."

Hearing this, the boy, once again, is four years old. His mother holds his hand so he won't fall from the low retaining wall where he balances.

"What is God, Mommy?" he asks.

She touches a leaf on a shrub next to the wall and tells him, "God is everything that is green and grows."

Fifty-two years later, at her deathbed, he holds her hand and cries for her and for the little boy he remembers. Two days later, she dies.

A Father's Letter, Fall 2016

Day by day, the sunrise moved from the north to the south of our neighbor's towering blue spruce. September brought the first blush of crimson and gold to the maple trees. By early October, there were the first signs of red and orange rose hips. As I had every year, I struggled alone with the more-than-one-hundred-pound weight of the oversized terra-cotta pot that held the tall white rose bush. I enjoyed the feeling of accomplishment when the container was once more in its place near the east-facing garage window, where the rose would lie dormant until spring.

On a weekend when the weather was right for staying indoors, I began the long-overdue task of sorting through one of the large folders of papers I had inherited. Everything was familiar to me until I came to a letter from my father written in the summer of 1976. He was sixty-two and I was thirty-three. It was eight years before Revelation Day II, when he and his sons would learn the truth about Sadie.

After reading a few paragraphs, I remembered that I had written him about my plans and dreams, and in return, he had written about what had been his own. In contrast to so many of my disturbing and painful memories of our relationship, as I read the letter, I felt embraced by the simple, eloquent way he conveyed the depth of his self-awareness, love, and hope for his children's happiness. Holding his letter in both hands, I reread it several times.

. . . If I can't remember my dreams, it's because that's all they really were is dreams. They lacked the person mature enough to even know if they were true desires or simply a child's dreams inspired by a loving, devoted mother who probably overindulged me and then became ill before she could help me know what course to follow and what it takes to really reach a goal. I'm happy now and try to be content with my life as it is, and not as I dream it should be or could have been or never will be. I get enormous satisfaction out of the growth of my three sons and my visions of their future. My life is almost too full and busy for me to have to live vicariously in their lives, but I am unhappy when they are in trouble, and I am in ecstasy when they are happy and productive. You have all been a source of deep gratification, and without the sure and comforting feeling of being loved by my sons, most all else would have little meaning, very little at all.

There was another sentence of powerful simplicity about why he was determined to build his own business: "I couldn't really get along with authority, I'm sure now in retrospect."

Those few words carried with them yet more memories, both ancient and recent. In the midst of reveling in my father's tender eloquence, I was reminded of several times I had witnessed his anger and aggression when he interacted with others who somehow caused him to feel belittled, dismissed, or humiliated. I also remembered a story he had told me about how, when he was a young man and before he had started his own business, he'd felt humiliated in some way by his supervisor, so he punched him, and was fired for it.

I was reminded of my own fear and anger when his temper would erupt at so many unexpected moments.

Punishment, Circa 1950

The boy has been sent to his room as a punishment, the same room he had been in when he cried inconsolably about the loss of his puppies. His father has hit the boy's upper arm, and it throbs. Though the boy is vague about the particulars, he is sure that he must have done something to deserve this.

As the voices and laughter of his parents and both of his brothers float from the backyard through the open window, he lies in bed, simulating first a whimper, then crying sounds, complete with gasping inhales and pathetic moans. He is determined that one of his parents will hear his whimpers and moans and run to absolve him of his childhood transgression. But, neither one of them does.

His little boy's way of coping is to believe that by falling out of bed, and making sure he lands on his sore arm, he can punish them and cause them to feel remorseful. The fall itself produces so little sound that he hardly hears it himself. So, he stomps his foot on the floor to simulate another fall. Even then, no one comes to help.

Seeking sympathy and forgiveness, he marches from his room and out the back door. "I fell out of bed and hurt my arm, the one that was sore."

So fervent to receive sympathy and forgiveness, he doesn't realize he could have accomplished his purpose by merely saying that he had fallen out of bed, instead of actually doing it.

The boy isn't sent back to his room. He's told he can get dressed and be with the family.

Punching a supervisor who had offended my father was his own creative way of *falling out of bed*, his own self-sabotaging way of responding to a capricious world that provided the chance for everything, from abundance and "ecstasy" to deprivation and sorrow.

Up to the end of his life, his "child's dreams" never took shape because, as he believed, his adoptive mother, Minnie, was too ill to help him. Reading his long-forgotten letter, I became more aware than ever before that his adoptive father, Saul, for whatever reasons, was not someone my father could or would turn to for the guidance and nurturance he longed for. I knew so very little about his relationship with Saul. There was not a word about him in the letter.

No wonder my father wanted only one song or hymn to be sung at his funeral, with the line he always said he loved: *Sometimes I feel like a motherless child . . . A long ways from home.* I leaned back against the cushion of the couch, feeling a depth of love for my father, the same kind of ecstasy, I imagined, that he had felt when he wrote about his sons. I thought about the terrible sequence of events that marked his life. Sadie died when he was but a boy of ten. A few years later, his "baby sister," with whom he shared a deep affection, was taken from him. Then, his adoptive mother, Minnie, died when he was but a young man of twenty-three.

In spite of this history, he became a successful and philanthropic businessman, a selfless friend, coach, scoutmaster, mentor, and confidant, esteemed by many throughout our city and beyond. All of this, even though his life had been, as he phrased it, "not as I dream it should be or could have been or ever will be."

I wanted to hold and comfort him, to be a father to him as he had been a father to me, so many times, in the ways that helped me the most.

An Apple Tree, Fall 1967

The boy has become a man in many senses, but still, when the woman he is living with says that they can't be together any longer, he calls his father, virtually paralyzed by the feeling of abandonment, the pain and depression.

"I'm so blue, I can't move," he tells his father.

"I could use some help pruning the apple tree," says the father. The tree has a trunk, of sorts, more the size of a heavy limb, not too much larger than the several horizontal ones, like arms raised in prayer for light and air. "Some of the branches are about to scrape the cars using the garage. Why don't you come over, and I'll wait until you get here."

Throughout the boy's life, his father's behavior had such a wide range, such wild swings between unexpected anger, even rage, all the way to the most sensitive and comforting expressions of love and support. Year after year, both of them have learned better how to behave to minimize the risk of conflict. On this day, the boy knows his father is the one person who will understand, who will give him the help he needs, whatever that should be.

They work together for the next hour, one of them with the pruner, one with the small handsaw. They hardly speak, but the boy feels protected by the silence, by the absence of unnecessary, even embarrassing, intrusions. There is no "You want to tell me what happened?" not even "I'm here if you want to talk about it." There is only a father who knows what his son needs, and a son who knows it will be that way.

When they finish their work, they nurse drinks and have a conversation. They stay away from the broken relationship and how much the boy dreads having to return to an empty apartment, where a kind of death has occurred. The worst part about being there will be fixating on where his ex-lover might be—and with whom.

It is late afternoon when he walks up to the second-floor apartment and pauses before turning the key in the lock. He pauses again before removing the key, and once more before turning the doorknob and taking the first step inside. The apartment that has always felt too small now feels empty and far too large. In a futile attempt to forestall the coming dark, he turns on all of the lights, as if that could assuage the pain that remains.

The boy does not feel the need to thank his father. He knows his gratitude has been conveyed without words, just as his father's love had been as they pruned the apple tree.

Winter 2017-18

December came and went, and it was my seventy-fifth January birthday. On that day, I had already lived five years longer than the too-short lifespan of my father. Throughout the winter, at unexpected moments, my thoughts drifted to how difficult it had been for me to unravel our complicated relationship. I recalled the day when, in my mid-twenties, a half century earlier, I had been regaling my therapist with stories of my father's magnificence.

"So, your father can walk on water?"

"Huh?"

Thus began the healing. It has been a slow, sometimes imperceptible, process until heart and mind could remain open to understanding life experiences in new ways. I needed to arrive at a place where my love and admiration of a father—gone now more than thirty years—could be expressed not just to camouflage my darker feelings. I have needed all of that time to cease repressing or denying what was painful and debilitating. Only then could I allow another reality to emerge and coexist. To heal has required embracing the "other" and transcending the limitations of being lost and drowning in the lonely "self." To heal has required relegating certain memories, photographs, and spoken words to a place called "that was then," and cradling close to the heart the ones that are called "and this is now."

Now, when I think of the person I was then, I imagine him on a path under a canopy of foliage, all veiled in a gray, pre-dawn fog. He isn't aware of my presence close behind him. He takes his last, unhurried step and comes to a halt, and I give the slightest of nods as I pass him. At the sharp bend in the path, I look back, just as beams of sunlight penetrate the canopy. In the light and warmth, he begins to dissipate along with the night fog. I watch until I see only green leaves glistening at daybreak.

Midsummer 2017

After a long, cool spring, the sun again rises on the north of the neighbor's spruce tree. As I write, I'm in the room where I keep that photograph of Sadie and her mother, Rose. I take the few pages of my father's letter from the desk drawer and lean them against the silver frame so they can share that place of prominence. What I don't have is a photograph of Minnie, nor do I recall having seen one. I've always wondered why that is. Should I find a photograph, there always will be room for it on the table.

In late afternoon, I leave my writing behind and walk outside. The oversized terra-cotta pot has been back in its place since early spring, and now the white rose bush is blooming, as is the rest of the garden. In the midst of this loveliness and tranquility, it takes only a few seconds for a perennial fantasy also to be in full bloom. In it, my father is alive, and I ask him to work with me in the garden— mine, not his. He welcomes the request, and I welcome his suggestions regarding the placement of new plants and the appropriate preparation of the soil.

At the end of the day, we sit on the patio, enjoy a glass of scotch, and admire our accomplishment: Not only has the garden been improved, but we've spent the day working as father and son without an angry word between us.

It waits until our second glass for me to tell him how much I learned as a boy and as a man during those times when we had been able to work and play together in peace. Then, I tell him that I have provided my children the chance to experience a garden's peaceful beauty, but never have demanded anything from them in return. I tell him that they, now adults, take pleasure in asking me which plants they should choose and how to care for them. They do this not because I am a gardener, but because I am their father. And now, I learn from them.

I know he understands everything he has heard from me because he gives one of his self-conscious laughs, more like a quiet clearing of the throat, revealing the depth of his emotions.

By the time I emerge from my fantasy, shadows have grown long and advanced across the patio and the garden and onto the lawn; but there is one more task to complete before dinner. I select the proper spade for transplanting a languishing rose bush, so it will receive the sun and nourishment it has been deprived of for too long. At the new site for the bush, I lift a handful of the loamy soil and inhale its clean, sweet aroma.

On this day, nothing eclipses my sense of well-being, not even as my foot presses on the shoulder of the spade and I remember standing at the side of my father's open grave and releasing a shovelful of earth onto his coffin.

Easter Sunday, 2019

Early spring snowfalls have given way to the first comfortable day for gardening. I begin by pruning winter damage from the transplanted rose bush that had been languishing two years earlier. Each of the main stems is loaded with buds varying in color from mid-red to red-scarlet. Dark green leaves of a close-by grouping of delphinium hug the ground, promising another season of abundance. Several of last summer's narrow bamboo supports for the delphinium remain and are tied with sisal twine, tangled and difficult to remove. I realize this is a task I should have dealt with last fall. In this moment of self-reproach, my father's sudden presence by my side doesn't surprise me. As I untangle the twine, he shakes his head just enough for me to notice. With falling intonation—that I understand to mean, *You should have done this months ago*—he says, "Hmmm," and is gone. With rising intonation—signifying an unexpected acceptance that some things endure—I conclude, "You haven't *changed*." Why, I wonder, am I at all surprised by my conclusion?

PART II

Legacy

What I hope to show is that to understand men's feelings
about love and work we need to understand our
unfinished business with our fathers.
—Samuel Osherson, Finding Our Fathers

JUST ANOTHER RITUAL

I pull the swinging cedar door, and we step into the merciless heat and humidity of a steam room. We are alone that day in 1975.

Father: "It's not hot enough in here."

Son: "It's too hot."

Father: "Only babies can't take heat. I'm staying on the high bench."

Son: "You're out of your mind. I'm moving to the low bench."

My father has invited me to join him at a Florida spa-hotel, so we can enjoy a few days together. I know he has been worried about me, as I have been experiencing a stressful transition in my domestic life. I am thirty-two; he is sixty-one.

The steam room is large enough for a half-dozen men, assuming no one were to lie down instead of sitting upright. It's imperative for me to begin on the upper bench. To do otherwise would be to ignore the first step of the time-honored "it's-not-hot-enough-it's-too-hot" ritual my father, my two brothers, and I (in various combinations, but always with our father) have observed many times in steam rooms, including this one.

A few minutes later, I retreat to the lower bench and hear my father say, "I was upset that a young man brought his five-year-old boy to the exercise class this morning. It was disturbing." His voice isn't angry; it's bewildered, even somewhat beseeching.

"For God's sake, Dad. How could that disturb someone unless he's already disturbed?"

"Because he was helping his son do the exercises, and it interrupted the class."

"And *that's* what disturbed you? You drive me absolutely crazy with this crap." Another one of those "here we go again" moments . . . I haven't expected this one, and it makes me angry . . . this is how we interact when each of us wants something from the other, and neither of us can ask for it in simple, direct words.

My father says nothing in response to my less-than-comforting comment. We change the subject and just relax.

The next day, he and I again sit alone in the not-hot-enough-too-hot steam room. From my perch on the bottom bench, I hear from the top bench, "I have it figured out."

Careful to leave the conversation door open, I say nothing.

"The father was so gentle and loving, I was jealous of the little boy. I couldn't admit it to myself, so I got angry at the father."

"It takes real courage to admit something like that, Dad."

I hear another one of his self-conscious laughs, the one that's more like a quiet clearing of the throat, the one that indicates he is flooded with emotion, and I'm content that he believes what his son has said to him.

And I, too, am flooded with emotion.

Did the father and son remind you of something you didn't receive as a boy? Are you ashamed of when you weren't the gentle father when I was a boy, frightened and hurt by you? You tell me this exercise-class story, and I think you want me to help you heal, while I want you to help me heal.

None of this do I say to him.

What I do say is, "You're right about one thing, Dad—it's not hot enough in here." I dip a ladle of water from the wooden bucket and pour it on the heated rocks. The hissing cloud of steam envelops me and obscures the room, but it doesn't obscure one crystalline thought.

Please, Dad. Let's just tell each other the truth, whatever it might be. The words can help heal both of us.

Later that day, I walk outside to where my father sits at a card table on the lawn and plays gin rummy with three other men. He and two others are shirtless, as are several of the spectators. Gray hair covers their chests and, on a few men, their backs. I laugh. First the steam room, now a group of silverback gorillas. This must be a mirage. The mountains of Rwanda look just like a manicured lawn in Florida. As I walk toward the men, I'm deep in a beautiful memory from seventeen years earlier, when I'm fifteen years old.

It was a Sunday afternoon, and my father asked me to take a drive with him, didn't tell me where, and I didn't ask. I was happy to be alone in the car with my dad. He parked on a main street lined with storefront businesses.

"Uh . . . Dad? It's Sunday . . . everything's closed."

"The cigar store isn't. C'mon."

A man inside the store saw us on the sidewalk, unlocked

*the swinging glass door, and pulled it open. He greeted my
father with, "Hi, Eddie." I liked it when people used "Eddie"
instead of "Edward." The small store, about twenty feet long
and wide, was filled with a sweet aroma of fresh tobacco.
Decorative boxes of cigars filled glass display cabinets and lined
the shelves that covered the walls. The man pushed a section
of the rear wall, and a hidden door swung open, revealing a
back room where a layer of cigar and cigarette smoke hung at
the ceiling, and middle-aged men were deep into gin rummy
games at five card tables.*

*My father took the open chair awaiting him. After at least
six years of having lost gin games to him at home and having
watched him play other people, I knew to move a chair from
the wall and sit behind and a bit to the side of him so I could
study his strategy. I could hardly believe what a damn cool place
this was to be with my dad. And no one said, "What's your boy
doing here, Eddie?" I wanted to say, but didn't, "Please . . .
somebody . . . I gotta have a cigar!"*

On the Florida lawn, I move a chair to my customary
place behind and a bit to the side of my father. He's in
the midst of what has been a long hand, marked by slow
decisions about each card played. His opponent discards a
deuce, and my father adds it to his hand. With a flourish, he
drops his gin card facedown on the table and says, "What's
the name of the game?"

Someone answers with an obligatory, "Gin." Then,
players and spectators alike examine the two hands of cards,
now faceup on the table, and begin the *patois*: "He should
have" and "I would have" and "Why'd he play the deuce and

not the jack," and more of the exchanges I have witnessed dozens of times, all part of the game, just another ritual.

"Great hand, Dad," I say.

He smiles at me. "Your old man hasn't lost his touch."

"Of course you haven't." I get up from my chair and say, "I'm going to take a nap, so I'll see you in the lobby before dinner." Not unlike bowing, I lean down to him as he stays seated, kiss his cheek, and walk across the lawn.

In the lobby a few hours later, my father and I greet each other and take a few steps toward the dining room. He stops and says, "After you left, one of the guys at the card table—right in front of everyone—said, 'You wanna know how lucky you are, Eddie? I have more money than I can spend, and I'd give away all of it, every damned penny, if my son would kiss me, just once, the way yours kissed you.'"

It might be more to himself than to me when my father finishes the story with, "Can you believe he said that?"

"Sure I can. What he said . . . and that he actually *said* it . . . is wonderful, don't you think?"

In this moment of intimacy with his son, yet again my father gives another of his self-conscious laughs. Yet again, I understand.

THE OTHER SIDE OF THE SCREEN DOOR

The weak can never forgive.
Forgiveness is the attribute of the strong.
—Mahatma Gandhi

A summer night, 1955. "Your friend Martin won't come into his own until his father dies."

I wondered why he had chosen that moment, right after a Boy Scout troop meeting as we stood by ourselves on the lawn of the grade school, to make his disturbing pronouncement. My father had been looking somewhere beyond me and seemed to be speaking more to himself, a forty-one-year-old scoutmaster, than to me, a twelve-year-old Boy Scout.

It would take many years after that night until I would understand that what he had offered me was his excuse, also an oblique apology, for the angry and sometimes abusive behavior I had experienced far too often as his young son. It was an apology that should have been made again—to his adult son—but never was, at least not in words like, *I'm sorry* or *I shouldn't have* . . . or *I wish I wouldn't have* . . .

Nine years after the evening on the grade school lawn, Martin Durvitch's father indeed did die. At a gathering of his family and their friends, I watched Martin's uncle place his hand on his nephew's shoulder and say, with a solemnity reserved for such occasions, "You're the only son. You have to take care of your mother and sister."

I didn't know if that hand on Martin's shoulder was there to comfort him or to control him. This scene—the Elder instructing the Younger—would have been familiar to our biblical ancestors, much of whose time was spent driving their flocks in search of green pastures. In Martin's case, much of his time was spent driving the used car he was so proud of in search of a Steak 'n Shake, or to and from more mundane places, such as high school.

When his uncle walked away, Martin said to me, in a hushed, almost monotone voice, "I'm selling my car. My family needs the money."

I didn't tell him what my father had said after our scout meeting. Whatever truth there might have been to his pronouncement, or if there had been none at all, Martin would have to discover it on his own, as I would have to do one day.

Fifty-one years after Martin's father died, another friend and I, two gray-haired men, continued our ongoing conversation about our families—especially our fathers.

"It's been thirty years since my father died," I said.

"Mine's been dead for years, too," Nick said. "He was pretty good at beating me when he was drunk, which was pretty regular. Sometimes he'd come into the bedroom I shared with my brother and wake us up, like his father had done to him pretty regular. I'd pretend to be sleeping. Sometimes this worked, and he'd deliver the beating to my brother instead of me."

"What'd your brother do?" I said.

"When my father left, my brother would beat the hell out of me."

We fell silent. In but a few ticks of the second hand of the clock on the wall, I'm once more the little boy.

At most seven years old, he's barefoot and in nothing but underpants, alone in his family's apartment. In the dining room, a shiny, brown cockroach stands guard like an enemy soldier, motionless. Terrified the cockroach will attack, he scrambles onto a dining room chair against the wall. He wants to smash the bug, or run to the safety of his bedroom. The one-inch monster scans the room with searching, threatening antennae, then races on its crooked legs across the tan pile carpet, squeezes through a crack between the floor and wall, and disappears. The little boy lowers himself to the chair seat and, as if checking the temperature of a bath, touches the carpet with the toes of his left foot. Summoning all his courage, he places both feet down and runs to his room. There he waits, trying to breathe.

Escaping from the memory of the cockroach, I said, "My father had outbursts of anger and violence that were frightening as hell, but nothing compared to the terror you experienced."

"Terror is terror, my friend. Don't try to compare them."

"I guess you're right, but . . ." I didn't finish the sentence. Again, it took no more than a few ticks of the second hand of the wall clock before I returned to a dream from thirty years earlier, when I was forty-two. Again, the little boy.

Trembling, he approaches the door from the dining room to the kitchen where the big man sits at the table that blocks the path to the outside and safety . . . he tiptoes into the room, his back sliding against the doorframe to stay as far away as possible from danger . . . he has to step closer to pass between the table and the refrigerator . . . the big man sits immobile . . . the boy sees that the man is his father . . . not the young, dangerous father, the soldier who returned a few years earlier from the war, but an old man . . . the boy chances to move so close to him that their faces almost touch . . . he sees that his father's eyes are covered with an opaque, gray film . . . he is blind, and he is thin and weak, but still might be dangerous . . . the boy runs the last few feet to the open kitchen door . . . he sees the metal staircase, other apartments, and the sky beyond them . . . only the wooden screen door blocks his way to safety . . . he fears the hook and eye will be too tight for him to open . . . he is able reach the hook that rests in an eye so big that a slight lifting of the boy's forefinger is all that is needed . . . he pushes the screen door, and steps outside. The dreamer awakes.

"Yeah, you're right about that, Nick. Terror is terror."

He leaned back in his reclining office chair just enough to swing his feet onto his desk. "I already came to a resolution of my feelings, and I've forgiven my father."

That was hard for me to believe, and I couldn't let it pass without commenting, "What kind of pronouncement is that? I have to try really hard not to dwell on my anger.

At any moment, a bad memory will return. When that happens, I try to focus on our love for each other. It's hard not to get hung up on the anger . . . mine, too, not just his . . . but I just don't wanna feed that beast."

While I continued my story, he leaned as far back as his chair would allow and locked his hands behind his head.

"Actually, my dad also was a remarkable guy," I said. "He helped so many people, even strangers. He was trying to grow his small business, but always found the time to coach our Little League teams and be our scoutmaster. My old friends still tell me how much he taught them and how much he helped them grow up. I mean, obviously, he did it for me, too."

Nick rolled his eyes, like he was looking for something on the perforated ceiling tiles. "I see. So you're saying your father was perfect?" I had heard a variation of that theme from the therapist, some years earlier.

"I guess that does sound like bullshit. When his anger would come at me . . . honestly, he was absolutely crazy. And it was terrifying. The worst part was not knowing when it would happen. The physical violence stopped when I was seventeen and we were in a really bad argument." I had been looking down at the carpet, so I paused only long enough to make sure Nick was still listening. "My father took a step toward me, and I just said, 'I'm warning you, Dad, don't even think about it.' He looked surprised, maybe a little afraid of me. He just turned and walked away, like he was relieved, like he also wanted all that crap between us to stop."

"You were lucky," Nick said. "My father didn't seem interested in stopping."

"I guess. But, the thing is, those times when my dad was in a rage, and sometimes I'd get hit, he'd never actually apologize. He'd be remorseful and express his love by doing one of those things we'd do when we hadn't been arguing. Like playing catch in the driveway. I was a good pitcher, and he'd wear this old catcher's mitt we had, and he'd have to put a sponge in the palm because I threw so hard. He never complained about it, but once in a while, he'd take off the mitt and shake his hand a few times, kind of like cooling it off. Other times, he'd bring me somewhere with him. Once, it was to an amazing cigar store, but that's a whole other story. Think how confusing it was, not being able to predict which father you'd be dealing with."

"Guess what?" He pulled the lever on his desk chair, and it forced him upright. "It's still confusing to me, and I'm fifty-seven years old."

"Yeah, pal, and I'm seventy-two. Plan on being confused for a lot longer."

All morning, I was thinking about the conversation I'd had with Nick a few weeks earlier. Now, it was Memorial Day, and feeling sorry for myself seemed much too self-indulgent when so many people were dealing with their own painful losses and haunting memories. Another friend was one of those people, a Vietnam veteran coping with lifelong physical and emotional healing from his devastating wounds. On this day of memories, I wanted to be close to him, someone who had struggled to find a way to forgive. So I called him.

"It's Memorial Day, and I've been thinking about you, Mark."

"I've been thinking about you, too. I'm really glad you called." He sounded very pleased, but also like he was preoccupied and tired. "I should've been in touch, but I've been immersed in a lot of stuff, some of it not so easy."

"I've been immersed in a lot of stuff, too, Mark. But you've had to deal with a lot more than I have."

"Oh? I don't know about that."

I was surprised that I had used that tired, old refrain. "You know what? I don't know about that, either." I knew I must have sounded pitiful. "Someone else delivered the same message the other day. 'Terror is terror.' Either one of you could have added, 'Cut the bullshit, and face reality.'"

"My point, exactly. I'm telling you, facing the wounds is the only way healing can happen."

A few days later, as we had planned during our phone conversation, Mark and I met at his favorite hangout where he ate breakfast every day. I walked into the café, and he stood up, flashing that big smile, and we hugged each other like long-lost brothers. He wore his customary jeans and, since the weather was warm, one of his customary T-shirts, this time in support of Veterans for Peace, a cause he held dear. His hair and thick walrus mustache were a bit longer and grayer, and a few of the wrinkles on his face might have been a bit deeper than when we were together a few months earlier.

Another day, another place, and once again I was one of two gray-haired men sitting together and continuing a conversation about their friendship and how to heal the wounds each had accumulated over his lifetime.

At the counter in the main dining area, Mark ordered his daily breakfast of eggs over-medium, toast, and coffee. I did the same, but my eggs were scrambled. When our breakfasts were ready, we carried our plates and coffee mugs through the door leading to a small area, more like a short, wide hallway with one table, which we chose. I watched with amused pleasure as he performed his ritual of pressing a fork into his eggs, first north and south, then east and west, producing a checkerboard of little yellow and white squares.

The bright yellow ones reminded me of something Mark had told me a couple of years ago. During an especially dark period of recovery, he lived alone in a warehouse of sorts, doing his best to resume his passion: painting and sculpting. One day, while walking toward the old industrial sink and carrying a plate with some of the leftover yolk from his fried eggs, he was thinking about how unattractive and demoralizing this whole scene was. As he did, he passed under a spotlight that illuminated the egg yolk and made it "glow a bright golden color that was absolutely beautiful. It was an epiphany. I just knew I was going to be okay."

Egg-cutting ritual completed, he looked at me and said, "When we first met, I was in bad shape, but I tried not to show it. I was in a deep forest, feeling completely alone, and somehow you understood, and you reached out to me. Honestly, because of that, I was no longer in the forest."

Our eyes remained locked together. "Truth is, Mark, I was in bad shape, too. There were days when I was feeling completely alone, not in a deep forest, but floating in a deep ocean. When I reached out to you, my hand was searching for a life raft."

"Yes, my friend. I understand."

"Yes, my friend. I know you do."

The two of us were ready to dig into our breakfasts, but struggled with the dumb, peel-off covers of those miniature plastic containers of strawberry jam for our toast. Watching each other bumbling through such a simple task, we laughed. Just happy little boys.

PULLING DOWN THE DARK

St. Louis, April 1981. The telephone rang at 7:30 A.M.

Father: Are you ready to meet?
Son: What? No, I'm not.
Father: Why not?
Son: How about it's seven thirty, Catherine and I just drove fifteen hundred miles, we got here late last night, both of us are sick, and we're sleeping.
Father: Let's get breakfast somewhere.

During the prior year, my father and I stood chest-deep in water, our arms draped over the side of a swimming pool, the hot sun on our foreheads. He said he knew I was worried about him and my mother. He reassured me they were doing fine, but acknowledged that the management of the business was beginning to tire them, and the people they had hired to assume the responsibilities weren't working out as well as expected. He added that he and my mother were capable of handling the situation themselves, and I should feel free to pursue my career plans. I said to him that it sounded like he was asking for my help, to which he said he probably was. Then, he added that he'd love it if I were to accept the offer. Had there been an uninformed eavesdropper sitting by the pool, the conversation between my father and me might have appeared to be a mature and loving interaction between father and son engaged in a rational conversation about the business. The eavesdropper probably wouldn't have concluded that underneath that interaction was a complex set of family dynamics, including unresolved, years-old conflicts. In retrospect, what comes to mind is I had taken my seat on a runaway train, but just sat serenely, looking out the window as if I were a tourist on vacation. What also comes to mind is, "For God's sake, what was I thinking?!"

Not long after the conversation at the swimming pool, Catherine and I sat with our Norwegian friends in a small alcove off the main room of their summer home on the Nesodden Peninsula. Each evening, we watched from the picture window as assorted vessels plied the waters of Oslofjord. Rivaling the wildflowers on the hillside, the summer night sky was a palette of purple, mauve, rose, blue, green, and shades in between. The colors were reflected in the clouds above and beyond the fjord.

This setting and the friendship among the four of us were so lovely and conflict-free that it's easy now to imagine I actually had been healthy enough to respond with a different answer to a question that I knew I'd soon be asked.

While the sky acquired deeper shades of colors, and the bottle of Johnnie Walker Red we had carried with us as a gift was less than half full, I spoke about the invitation to join our family's business. As I knew he would, Mike asked the question that took all of us out of the beauty of our surroundings and back into the world of work and doubt and family struggles.

"Why in hell would you want to leave where you and Catherine live in New Hampshire? Both of you would have to give up the great work you're doing. Why would you sacrifice that to relive so much of the unpleasant part of your family experience to work with your father? And your mother?"

"I really don't know, Mike," I said, "but, I think I should do it. You probably think I'm out of my mind." I might have been. I had begun to feel like one of my advisees from my earlier teaching days, seeking guidance from the wise professor—but doing a good job resisting it.

Early February 1981. "Don't do us any favors," was my mother's response when I called to tell my parents that Catherine and I had decided to move to St. Louis. In spite of that absurd response—which, alone, should have been enough for us to reverse our decision—we left New Hampshire in April, driving past lakes and ponds still frozen with thin layers of ice. At the end of a two-day trip, we arrived late at night during a rainstorm more like a monsoon. And both of us had caught terrible colds during the drive.

It didn't surprise me, and probably didn't surprise anyone else, that within the first month of our living in St. Louis, it was as if we had placed a clear plastic overlay, FAMILY, over a poster board, BUSINESS, making it more than difficult to distinguish one from the other. No one, I least of all, could maintain a proper boundary between them.

During that first month, I took a few days off of work so Catherine and I could consider, without interruption, whether we should return to New Hampshire or go somewhere else. Almost daily, we questioned the wisdom of our move to St. Louis. The stress of my relationship with my father and, to a lesser extent, my mother, was what Mike had predicted would happen.

In spite of how dissatisfied Catherine and I were with the situation we were in, we decided to stay. I'm certain that had I said we should leave, it wouldn't have taken us long to pack. To this day, I'm overwhelmed by the love and generosity Catherine exhibited in supporting what I said I wanted. I'm overwhelmed not only by my flawed thinking, but by my selfishness, as well.

It took another two months before my father and I decided we should have dinner at a restaurant so we could talk about what he knew was my growing sense that I had made the wrong decision to leave New Hampshire. While we ate, I told him that the constant tension between us, and my perception that we were so often on the verge of an argument, was making it next to impossible for me to continue working in the business.

"Please stay," he said.

"I don't know if I can . . . or should."

We both knew that this encounter had the potential for making him feel dependent and weak, and unable to continue a conversation without expressing his anger. Yet, this time, he beat back those feelings.

"Please stay."

Ambivalence consumed me. I didn't know if I wanted to love him or punish him for all the years when I was a child living with his anger that sometimes led to violence. In truth, I must have wanted to do both. I also seemed to have wanted the same regarding my mother, for her impulsiveness and unpredictability, both of which I experienced as her style of aggression. And how could I forget what I thought had been her failure to intervene effectively, if at all, when my father's anger and violence erupted?

And yet, I stayed, and Catherine stayed with me.

A family business is no place for someone who harbors those complex feelings, many of which hadn't been explored to a depth they warranted. They were damaging ballast; the unconscious mind alone can prompt some very destructive behaviors. I have little doubt that some of my dismal performance contained a childish and destructive form of retribution, a way of hurting others and, in the process, myself. The situation had become even more complicated because of disagreements with my two brothers who weren't working in the business but had percentages of ownership that I was in the process of purchasing from them.

March 7, 1985. Four years had passed since Catherine and I moved to St. Louis, and many of my father's and my old wounds remained unresolved and continued to hurt both of us. While my parents were away on vacation, I had breakfast with the company's attorney to discuss not so much my growing sense that I should disengage with the business, but to vent my feelings to someone who also worked with his father.

"I really can't stand working with him any longer," I said to the attorney. "The stuff with my father and me is exhausting, and my mother drives me nuts, even if she doesn't work there any longer. Honestly, I'd be happier if they just didn't come home." As soon as I said those words, they were as unappealing to me as my half-eaten breakfast. I used my fork to push around what remained on my plate, remembering the phone call just two days before this breakfast.

I'd called my father at the hotel where he and my mother stayed during their late winter vacation in Florida. We talked for a few minutes about his exercise routines in the gym; then we moved to the family business itself. I was pleased by its current performance and was pleased to be helping, in spite of how conflicted I continued to feel about being involved.

"Everything's okay here, Dad. We've done well, the numbers are great, and you've got nothing to worry about. Just enjoy yourselves."

"I thought about you last night," my father said, "and I have to tell you about it. I was in bed, and the room was completely dark. I saw your face in front of me, and I said to you, 'I can rest for the first time, because you're there taking care of the business.'"

What he said was so touching I wanted to preserve the feeling, to avoid having it ruined by anything else either of us might say.

"I really do love you, Dad. But, we should get off the phone now."

"Why? What's wrong this time?"

"What you said was beautiful. We should quit before we ruin it with an argument."

He was silent, but I could hear him smiling in the dark. "Goodbye, Dad."

First, on the telephone with my father, then at breakfast with the attorney. Two conversations, two days apart, that captured the essence of my ambivalence: wanting to embrace and be embraced, and wanting to be free from that embrace.

In the parking lot outside the restaurant, the attorney said he'd call me in the afternoon so we could talk further. Someone else called first.

When I walked into my office, a colleague told me she had taken a call from a doctor in Florida and left his phone number on my desk. "Your father hurt his leg, is what he told me." We gave each other a you-don't-believe-it-either look.

I read the phone number, studied it for a moment to avoid placing the call, then did.

"Mr. Hopper? Are you the next of kin?"

"To whom?"

The phone call disconnected. I called again.

"I'm an emergency room physician at the hospital in Miami. I have bad news for you. Your father has passed away."

While I had been pushing around the remains of an unappetizing breakfast and wishing my parents wouldn't come home, my father had died.

The news was devastating and disorienting, but not

surprising. I immediately recalled a conversation from four years earlier, during my first year of working in the business.

I leave the table while others of the extended family linger over dessert. My father joins me in the living room, and we sit next to each other on upholstered chairs; he leans toward me and speaks not much above a whisper so no one can hear us. I know to do the same.

"I've had pains. I think you'll have to learn the business more quickly than we thought."

My reflexive response is an inappropriate "Dad, please . . . what the hell are you talking about? I saw you've been limping. What happened?"

"Don't tell your mother. Promise?"

"Yeah. Sure."

"I jumped off the roof and twisted my knee."

"You what?"

"I was checking the AC unit."

"And you didn't climb down the ladder you must have used to climb ten feet up?"

"I just felt like jumping."

"And that's *why I need to learn the business quickly? Because you twisted your knee?"*

"I have pains in my chest. I know what they mean."

"And you decide to tell me this now, with all the family sitting in the other room?"

"It's been on my mind."

"Your mind? And you haven't seen your doctor what's-his-name, right?"*

"I already know what I need to know."

I suggest that a more reasonable response might be a discussion of treatment options, including bypass surgery, and he says, "No. I don't want to be an invalid walking around like an old man, all bent over."

In a small act of mercy, he doesn't do pantomime.

There had been an intimate, gentle character to the conversation, but I wondered if it had been a camouflaged version of one of his old, disturbing themes: the son becomes a man only when his father dies. I first had heard it as a twelve-year-old Boy Scout, but on that night, he was talking about one of my closest friends and his father.

Not long after the phone call with the emergency room physician, I was on an airplane to Florida with my younger brother to bring our mother home. During the flight, we imbibed enough of those little bottles of scotch for the flight attendants to suggest we stop. They were, of course, the same attendants who had provided us with those little bottles.

We took a taxi from the airport to the hotel, where we met with our father's close friend, Bishan, an expert trainer who came from a family of yogis. He recounted how the death had occurred. They had just finished a strenuous exercise routine, and, in typical fashion, my father said he felt great and wanted to do the routine again. He didn't know he had only a few seconds left to live.

Concerned that my father was overdoing his exercises, Bishan turned away and pretended to adjust the controls on the device that played Indian music, hoping that his student's urge to continue would subside. It did, but not in the way Bishan had hoped. He heard the thud of a body collapsing onto an exercise mat and turned to see his friend lying there, dead.

I knew he had died in a way he would have wanted to die: in the gym, enjoying himself, and not *an invalid, walking around like an old man, all bent over.*

He was seventy years old. I was forty-two.

The next day, my brother and I did bring our mother home to St. Louis, after having arranged for our father to make the same journey late that night. Her sister stayed with her, and my brother and I went to our own homes. A close friend of our family offered to meet the funeral parlor staff at the airport and remain with them until they would arrive at the mortuary.

From where Catherine and I lived, we could hear occasional airplanes on their landing approaches, especially on quiet nights. Around eleven o'clock, we tried to sleep, but only lay on our backs, listening for my father's plane, scheduled to arrive soon. A few minutes after eleven, we heard its engines. They grew louder, and I felt like an inanimate weight sinking deep into the mattress while my father floated effortlessly above. Motionless, we listened until the sounds of the engines faded to nothing.

I gave the eulogy at the funeral service. We buried my father, but I couldn't lay to rest certain questions that still troubled me. When I visit him at his grave, do I tell him that I, too, had a vision before he died, but it wasn't of his loving face in front of me in the dark? Instead of saying something to him as touching as his "I can rest for the first time," do I tell him, instead, that I had wished he wouldn't come home?

Would I hear him answer, "It's okay, son. We can talk about it," or would I hear the earth moan beneath my feet?

St. Louis, 1987. Catherine and I eloped—if that's the right word for a wedding only a mile or so from where we lived. Other than ourselves, the only people who knew about the wedding were another couple, good friends who fulfilled the requirement of two witnesses. Afterwards, the four of us enjoyed an elegant lunch at their home. Before leaving for the ceremony, they had prepared their home for a wedding celebration: white embroidered tablecloth, fine crystal and china, and delectable salads and wines. Their newborn son slept peacefully in the next room.

After lunch, a cold rain began as we drove toward the airport to leave for a brief honeymoon. We decided to stop at the cemetery to tell my father we were married, and to imagine his blessing. This was a day of celebration, not a day of apologies for things I had wished for on the very day he died. As we neared the cemetery, I was thinking about an evening eight years earlier.

Catherine and I are in St. Louis to attend my younger brother's wedding. The night before the ceremony, a dozen celebrants meet at a restaurant where we eat and drink for hours. At one point in the evening, my father and I find our way to the men's room and stand next to each other at the urinals. It reminds me of childhood when my brothers and I would stand at the toilet and aim our streams in a game we called "Crossing Swords." I try, once again, to understand that childhood game, and know that it will be of no use to ask my brothers to explain it. Though both of them are psychoanalysts, they will be of no help at all.

My father and I say nothing until we are at the sink washing our hands and smiling at each other's reflection in the mirror.

"Are you going to marry Catherine?"

"I believe so," I say, noting his moist eyes.

"I want you to marry Catherine."

"Dad . . ."

"I want to be there."

"Okay, Dad."

"And I want to see your children."

"And I want you to see them, too. I want them to know you."

Later that night, after the party, I tell Catherine what happened, and she says that earlier in the day, he placed his hand on hers. "I want you to marry my son," he said.

When we arrived at the cemetery, the gate was locked. I had forgotten it was one of the Jewish holidays, and tradition demands that the cemetery should not be visited during those particular days. We climbed over the low stone wall, told my father we had married, and knew he would be pleased. We placed a small rock on his headstone and climbed back over the fence. In our car, we laughed about how wet, muddy, and happy we were on our wedding day.

Two years later, on January 7, 1989, our son, our firstborn, was delivered on his and my forever-to-be-shared birthday. I became a father at forty-six. Catherine had been in premature labor, which resulted in her having to spend the last four months of pregnancy in bed at home, on her left side, allowed to get up only to walk to the bathroom and to shower, or travel by wheelchair-automobile-wheelchair to the hospital for periodic doctor visits. But for the emergency and long-term medical care at the hospital, and the loving support of family and friends, we might not have been parents of our boy.

On an evening when Michael was almost two, I entered our front door after a long day of work and heard Catherine and him talking in the kitchen. I felt so happy hearing their voices, I didn't take the time to remove my coat before walking toward them, but I did remember to be careful. A month earlier, Catherine had said—and not for the first time—that from the moment I began working with my father, and even after he died, I often would come home in a sullen mood. "That happens more times than you might realize," she said. "You come home like you said he used to do. I know you don't want to look that way, but you do."

I was ashamed by the truth of what she said. It was intolerable for me to imagine subjecting our son, as well as our expected second child, to the disturbing behavior I had been subjected to, and to imagine becoming someone they might one day wish would not come home. When I was a boy, then a teenager, and even when visiting during breaks in college, sullen was the mood my father often brought home, especially during periods when the business was struggling. Anticipating his arrival as darkness was approaching, my stomach would tighten. I was afraid that an argument between us would be moments away. And sometimes it was.

That was the kind of father I never wanted to be. I wanted to be like the father who had said he wanted to meet my children, the father who had told Catherine he wanted her to marry his son, the father whose blessing we sought on our wedding day.

Those were my thoughts as I walked into our kitchen, where Michael was standing on a chair and he and his mother were mashing potatoes in an almond-colored porcelain bowl.

"Daddy's home!" Michael shouted, smiling and reaching for me. I scooped him into my arms and held him close. He laughed as I kissed his neck and nuzzled my chin against the soft skin of his cheek, as my father had done with me all those years ago.

I always loved the feel of his chin whiskers against my cheek and the mild aroma of his cologne. Even as a young child, I understood he was being careful not to press hard enough for his whiskers to hurt my soft skin. When I was a grown man, and my father and I hugged, I still loved feeling those whiskers against my cheek.

Holding our son against my body with my left arm, I kissed Catherine and patted her stomach and our second child within.

"I'll tell you something remarkable that happened a little while ago," she said. "Michael climbed onto this chair so he could help me with the potatoes. Right, Michael?" Our boy smiled at his mother as I held him close. "He opened the drawer on the cabinet under the counter and took out that skinny, stainless steel tube for steaming milk . . . you know, the one that fits into the espresso machine."

"What was he doing?"

"He held the tube and reached the curved end toward the ceiling. He did it several times. I asked him, 'What are you doing, sweetheart?' and he said, 'Pulling down the dark, so my daddy will come home.'"

"Michael said that? You said that, Michael?" I stopped myself from crying with happiness; I didn't want our toddler son to see tears he might misunderstand at this precious moment. He laughed again as I tickled his neck with my chin, then handed him back to Catherine. I walked to our living room and sat on the couch, thinking about what just happened. The gathering darkness felt more like dawn.

After a few minutes of sitting alone, I returned to the kitchen and was bathed in the light and warmth of my growing family, and the aromas of dinner. Mine was a better feeling than any I ever had known.

February 1991. That feeling became even better a few months later, when our daughter, Caroline, was born. I felt complete in a way that I always had hoped I would feel. The births of our children were a deliverance to the next plateau of adulthood, a high diving board where I stood with my toes hooked over the edge, suspended somewhere between fear and excited anticipation.

Before either of our children had been born, I was a member of a business group that served a number of functions, including being an informal advisory board for each member. I had made a half-hearted attempt to participate in the support group, though I needed the guidance the members could offer. The group included owners of profitable businesses in real estate development, home furnishings, restaurant chains, professional placement services, trucking, and more. I tended to ignore their advice while my own business deteriorated as a result of my incompetence as the owner and senior executive.

There always was at least one woman in the group, yet I experienced the attitudes and behaviors of the members, each of whom was a strong and competent owner/operator, as typically "masculine." I assumed the others in the group perceived me as weak and inadequate, what they might have termed "feminized." I do admit that the word crossed my mind, and I didn't like the feeling.

As the comments of the group piled up like logs encountering an obstruction on their way downstream, I recognized I was angling for my colleagues' approval, even as I was appalled by much of what they said and how they said it. Then, when our first child was born, the consensus was that I was an irresponsible businessman for staying home from work as much as I did. One person said I wasn't committed to my business because it was more important to me to be with our child than to be at the office. Another said I was using the birth of our child as an excuse for staying home from work.

Ignoring that he was, in part, talking about my relationship with the business, I was appalled by his comment. "Can't you see it's a *reason*, not an *excuse?*" I said. "Staying home with a new baby is something *bad?* Are you *serious?*"

During one meeting, the members reached their limit of tolerance for my ambivalence about being in the group and in business itself. They told me to get out of the business of business and do something I love. "Go back to being a professor," one of them said with self-confident ease, including a flick of the wrist that I experienced as "Someone, remove this peasant from my court."

I'm a teacher, young and confused. Before me sits a student in his early twenties, soft-spoken, seeking my advice. He tells me he doesn't know what to do in a few short months after graduating. I don't tell him that I don't know what I want to do, either. We talk about what motivates people to make certain career choices, and I can't tell whether this young man is the most relaxed person on Earth or the most passive. I ask for the second time what he thinks he'd like to do. Without any trace of humor or irony, he says he wants to be a "petty" bureaucrat. Says he wants to be part of a large organization and have a job "I can do." I don't know how to help him, though I'm moved by how comfortable he appears to be and how different he is from many of his fellow students consumed by ambition. I offer him a few simplistic and not very helpful observations about organizations. He thanks me as he leaves.

Another member of the business group at the table asked, "If you could do whatever you want, what would you do?"

Aware that my answer would be provocative, I said, "I'd spend my time helping catch Nazis before they die." Indeed, that was one of the things I hoped I would do in the near future.

He laughed, looked upward, raised his hand, and

quickly clenched it into a fist, the way he would to catch a flying bug. Instantly, I was out-of-body, looking down from a perch near the ceiling, watching myself getting angrier and more defensive. He repeated his offensive gesture, and I said nothing—at least not out loud. Had I spoken my thoughts at that moment, the group would have heard, *And this guy and I are the only Jews in this group? If there's a God in heaven, could He possibly have created this fucking moron?*

Descending from my perch near the ceiling and reoccupying my place at the table, I said something else I knew would be provocative, though true. "What I really feel is that I never want to be in a position where I have to work for one of you."

I knew where it came from: the story about how my father couldn't get along with authority, and how he had punched his supervisor. At least in the retelling, he acknowledged he regretted what he had done. I wondered if I would have the same feeling one day about what I had just said.

At the business table, the others stared at each other with big, round lemur eyes, as if they couldn't believe I had said what I'd said, and as if they didn't have the same sentiment that I had expressed about working for anyone else in the group. What I presumed was their pretense made me even more agitated.

"Also, I don't want my children to grow up and have to work for your children."

"What an odd comment," Barbara said.

"That's bullshit, Barbara. Don't tell me you want your daughter to work for my son or daughter, instead of the other way around."

"I wouldn't mind."

"And I wouldn't mind believing you if in fact I did—but I don't."

No lemur-eyed stares this time. They just shook their heads. I thought about acknowledging that I might be wrong about Barbara, since I had no idea what her children or ours would think about working for each other.

I might have gained the approval I sought from them and, more importantly, some much needed counsel had I just admitted that I was embarrassed by my predicament, instead of giving a defensive and provocative response to an appropriate question: "If you could do whatever you want, what would you do?"

Had I been more willing to acknowledge my obvious failures, I would have told them what I knew was the truth. I would have said, "Whatever I'll choose to do remains a mystery to me, as it has all of my life. All I know is that I made a terrible mistake trying to be a businessman, especially in my own family's business. I need your help to salvage this situation in the best way possible. I owe that not only to myself, my wife, and our children, but also to so many other people."

Later in the year, I sold the business in a transaction best described as financially disastrous. Following the sale, I did my best to help shelter our young family of four. Catherine and I, after much discussion, decided we should deplete our resources, if necessary, so our children could have both parents at home with them as long as possible. We bought an older home, which I constantly repaired. I helped take care of our son and daughter by changing diapers (as well as anyone); reading to them and then with them; painting pictures together in the garden on our makeshift easels; teaching them how to carve Halloween pumpkins; gardening in a way that included them; and volunteering at the Children and Parents Family Center, where I served a term—more like a jail sentence—as recording secretary. I remained a not-so-good cook, and didn't spend much time practicing to be better.

Being with our children as much as I was every day helped me in my search for direction, meaning, and structure. It was uncertain what the outcome of the process would be, but I wanted it to include a way of earning money that didn't require me to live someone else's ideal of what it was to be successful in our society.

It was painful to admit at the time, and uncomfortable even now to reveal, but as a still-new father, there was one reason why I felt relieved that my own father was dead. His death made it easier for me, in caring for my family, to commit errors and forgive them, and achieve successes and take pride in them, rather than fixating on whether my efforts would have found favor in my father's eyes.

There had been a very special moment during a very special day in 1992, when our son was almost three, our daughter almost one, and I was anticipating my all-too-soon forty-ninth birthday. Early in the morning, I was sitting in my usual chair, reading a book, when I experienced a strong, though undefined, urge to get up and move. Pacing through the house, I felt excited, but wasn't sure why.

I walked to a large mirror and stood in front of it, imagining my father's reflection next to mine, as it once had been in another mirror when he had said he wanted to live to see Catherine's and my children. I looked at him and thought about some of the difficult things—among the many that were good and nurturing—that had happened between us.

In a moment, my reflection was alone in the mirror. I leaned closer and studied the wrinkles and creases in my face, and my graying, thinning hair. But none of that mattered. What I cared about was living longer than my father's too-short life of seventy years. What I cared about was being here for my children, and being nothing but gentle and nurturing as I helped them along their paths to adulthood.

And I always have been.

The early years of fatherhood were filled with wonder and pleasure beyond what I could have imagined. Nevertheless, those years were not without stress and self-doubt. Deep in remorse over the loss of savings and income, and agonizing over how soon our funds would be depleted, I spent much of my time sorting out what I would do next to earn a living.

Often, I would self-medicate by watching television. On a day that was nothing out of the ordinary, I stopped channel surfing in the midst of an interview of a woman who had been born a man, then underwent surgery to transform his, to be her, body. When she spoke of "shedding a skin" that had been covering the "true person within," I connected with her at once.

As different as our life stories had been, each of us was experiencing a transition, indeed a transformation, though

she seemed much farther along in a more complex process
than mine. For ten years in business, I had donned a suit
of clothing that on most days felt constrictive, a skin to be
molted and replaced by a new one. The challenge I faced
was to fashion that new skin with a look and comfortable fit
that had eluded me. It would happen gradually, not at once
as it might elsewhere in the animal kingdom.

Within a few months of my father's death, he had
appeared standing before me in a dream. I placed the palm
of my right hand on his bare chest and felt the thick hair
beneath my fingers, the gray hair I always had hoped I
would have on my own chest. We said nothing. I looked at
his face. He looked past me. I awoke.

While Catherine slept at my side, I lay in bed, just as
I had when we waited to hear the plane bringing home
my father in his coffin. But this time, I felt a lightness
throughout my body and in my spirit. I could still feel on
my palm and fingertips the hair, the skin, and the muscles
of his chest. And I loved him.

I loved him.

Dreaming, I had wanted the comfort of his presence,
to absorb some of his strength by touching him with my
open palm upon his bare chest. But even in the dream, I was
aware that the placement of my hand was also how you keep
someone at a distance, out of your own territory. Awake, I
still wanted to be near him, to be able to touch him. But, if
that were possible, I knew I mustn't let him in, at least not
in the way I had before.

Had I been a wolf, I would have marked the boundary
of my territory.

Months passed, and the trepidation that accompanied the wearing of manhood and fatherhood was sometimes challenging enough for me to become again the anthropologist I had trained to be. I began to feel a kinship with men far from where I dwelled. My thoughts, at times, brought me to the Dani tribesmen of New Guinea, and their simulated clan warfare and violent ambushes on trails near their villages. At other times, my thoughts were of Siriono men in the Amazon rainforest, under constant pressure to feed their family's insatiable hunger by successful hunting with longbows.

Roaming the concrete rainforest of suburban St. Louis, I would smell the barbecue grills and see the shirtless males standing before their fires, basting the meat of monkeys, peccaries, tapirs, and birds I couldn't identify, as their wives and children huddled together, hoping the family would eat before darkness arrived, along with fearful things of the night.

There's a time-worn truth that relationships don't end at the moments of formality and ritual, such as funerals or divorce decrees. They change in character and meaning sometime before or after those formalities, when people's thoughts and behaviors shift in fundamental and enduring ways. Sometimes, they never end at all.

It's been thirty-five years since that dream of my hand on my father's chest. I'm seventy-seven now, and continue to examine my father's and my relationship. So, I ask, when does someone truly die? When does a father die? When is it that a son becomes a man? When does he wear his own skin?

During those contentious meetings with my business group, there was something I wish I had revealed, whether or not they would have respected it. I was feeling too insecure and defeated to explain, without anger or defensiveness, that I wanted to work at something that made me feel as pleased as I had felt on a day, long ago, in a small park near the college I attended.

The two of us, she in her fourth year, I in my second, sitting close on a picnic table, our feet on the bench, the fall afternoon sun warming our backs. We are deep in conversation, and when she says, "You remind me of a bard, wandering the countryside reciting poetry," my eighteen-year-old, romantic self wants to believe her. I will never see her again after she graduates, nor will I ever forget that day.

Four years ago, on a cold Thursday evening, I drove to my first session at what is known as a "roundtable," a critique group for writers. Each person was to read her or his writing, and the others were to provide oral and written feedback. With each passing mile, "critique" began to function less as an adjective or noun, and more as an intimidating, transitive verb with a direct object: my words—and me.

In spite of mounting apprehension about exposing my imperfections, and in spite of being aware that I've never been a bard wandering the countryside—except in my imagination—I felt ready to hear and benefit from the comments of my new colleagues.

When it was my turn, the group leader reviewed the rules that each person at the table must follow: no apologies, excuses, or explanations.

Just read.

"It was the silence of Jerusalem and its surrounding hills and villages that I remember most of all." Reading that simple sentence was exhilarating. It was a pinch of my forearm, confirming I was in my own skin.

At this table, no one asked, "If you could do whatever you want, what would you do?"

At this table, there was no need to explain.

Just be.

ARENA

Of my bed every morning out I jump
Ready for the fields of life to go
Armor, sword and spear in hand
Into survival's arena myself I throw
—*Demetrios Trifiatis, "The Gladiator"*

Fall 1958. Our family's dinner table. My parents had invited Rolf to join them and my two brothers and me, and each passing moment of the conversation added another layer to my dread. Rolf, a Dutch exchange student—who could have begun college at home instead of being bored at our high school—and my older brother—already in his second year of college—were discussing each other's professional aspirations. Rolf didn't say "a lawyer," he said, "a legal scholar." My older brother said, "a sociologist."

I knew that at any moment, it would be my turn.

As if on cue, Rolf looked across the table and said, "And you, Myles? You want to be an athletic coach, yes?" as if he were asking, "And what do you want to be when you grow up?"

I'm sixteen. Leave me alone. Oh, God, I know he remembers I told him about my older brother's dog when we were kids. A tulip-shaped, white blaze on her forehead. Hundreds of millions of tulips in Holland, and I asked if he knows what a tulip is. The same smile he's giving me now.

"Yes, I do," is what I said, but didn't know if I even believed it. This was my script. I was locked into it, having to remain in character and perform as the academic low achiever, an ignorant child, compared to Rolf and my older brother.

Someone say something . . . tip over a glass of water . . . anything to shift the attention from me. If I say I want to be a student like the two of you, they'll laugh . . . then they'll continue their discussion of law and sociology.

And that's exactly what these two intellectual high achievers did. I remember nothing they discussed, except that it felt to me as if they'd been careful to include footnotes and citations.

~ ~ ~ ~ ~

A football season, that same year. My coach and role model smoked a crazy contraption of a pipe with a stem that sported a twisted metal tube to cool the air and smoke that he inhaled into his lungs and exhaled from his nose. Against team rules, I bought a pipe, smoked it a few times using the same brand of tobacco—Prince Albert in a can—and exhaled through my nose.

In our second game that year, I injured my right knee. The pain was so intense it was a bright white silence. There was considerable inconvenience being encased in a cast from hip to ankle, requiring me to use crutches, but I actually was relieved to be off the field. It was an honorable way to resolve my ambivalence about having an identity I feared would be indelible: "Athlete. Not good student."

When the cast was removed a month later, I began to run with the team during practice, but only in straight lines, fearing to make a sharp turn on a damaged knee. I ran because I didn't know how to stop. I ran because I didn't know how to answer my persistent question, the one that defined my internal struggle: If I stop running, what books would I read?

I was unable to play the rest of the season.

Fall 1959. My last year of high school would begin in two weeks, as would our first game. At a practice, I jogged on the infield, just inside of the quarter-mile cinder track, and watched the tops of my shoes as they hit the turf—over and over. It felt like my cleats weren't biting into a solid field of play, like it might feel in an earthquake when *terra firma* liquefies.

I noticed two boys, classmates, non-athletes and writers for the school paper, playing catch with a football at the top of the bleachers. Everyone knew they were destined to attend high-status universities.

I want to be like them . . . I hate running like this . . . the co-captain of the team, the quarterback, wants . . . say it, if only to yourself . . . to quit . . . How can I tell anyone that I'm running because I don't know what books I would read if I stop?

In the third game, I did make a sharp turn. The pain was another bright white silence. Struggling to stand up and hobble off the field, I wondered what all of this running and football and pain had been worth. What a waste it had been. I knew this was the end.

I never played on a sports team again.

The high school world continued, students walked back and forth in the hallways and up and down the stairs, and Miss Helen Dyer continued to demand that we pronounce every French word as the French do. By "the French," she meant "Parisians." By way of convincing us how serious she was about pronunciation, she inserted the eraser end of a pencil into her mouth and closed her lips. When she removed the pencil, her lips remained in a small, open circle, as if they were puckered for a kiss. She told us to do the same. "Now, say the letter 'e.' This, and only this, is the proper way to pronounce a French 'u.'"

She never allowed our lesson to continue until anyone who had made an error in pronunciation corrected it. Often, we practiced the correction over and over until she was satisfied. I wasn't an outstanding student of the French language, but my pronunciation was *magnifique et formidable*.

After a typical class, Miss Helen Dyer stopped me as all of us were filing out of the room. "Stay for a minute. I want to talk to you about something important," she said. We sat at desks next to each other. "I worry for you. You must find something to replace what you've lost. If you don't, I'm afraid you'll suffer, and I don't want that to happen to you. Why not consider the theatre and acting? You'd be good at it."

I thanked her, said I'd think about her advice, and left the room elated. I did as Miss Dyer recommended and was a cast member in several plays during that last year of high school, and for years thereafter. And I loved that in theatre there were new kinds of coaches—awesome coaches, like Miss Dyer, and the theatre faculty members. We read and memorized books together. We learned stage directions and how to coordinate our movements. We practiced and sweated, and practiced and sweated some more. We were a team.

And one of my favorite teammates was Carol. She had a special way of tilting her head to one side or the other when she offered her shy smile. When I think of that smile, it reminds me of the smile my mother often used, though I don't think of her as shy. There was something about Carol that was comforting and supportive, though I sensed in her voice what seemed to be a pedal note of sadness. I think it might have been that note of sadness more than the shyness that reminded me of my mother.

It was as if Miss Dyer had set another dinner table and provided me with at least one part of the answer to Rolf's question were he to ask me again: "No, not a coach, but I really do love the theatre. By the way, there's a Saturday matinee you might want to attend."

In late fall, a guidance counselor who liked me contacted someone she knew at Colorado College and told him they should admit this young man. To my surprise, they did. I had applied to only one other school, and it rejected me. *That* wasn't a surprise. I'd applied there because the wastebasket in my room had images of college pennants, and I liked the one from the University of Southern California. Even more, I liked the cheerleaders I had seen on television.

During the summer before I left for Colorado, I had surgery on my knee. I can't remember how long it was before I entered the hospital that my father revealed what had occurred the day of my first injury. At halftime, while he waited for me outside the locker room, he overheard the coach say, to my closest friend and teammate, that he wished he had his quarterback from the team he had coached before coming to our school. This infuriated my father, and as he would have done in any situation like this one, he turned and walked to where the coach and my friend were standing. "My son's injured, and you're telling his best friend that you wish you had your former quarterback? And you call yourself a coach?"

When he told me what happened, I overcame my immediate impulse to be infuriated with him for berating my coach. A moment later, my feeling changed to admiration for what he had done, and I told him so. I admired his fierce loyalty and impulse to protect his sons. I have no recollection if my father told me, or even if I asked, what my coach might have said or done after being confronted in that way.

As I lay in the hospital a couple of days after surgery, the coach arrived. His visit was unexpected, but I was pleased to see him. It was gratifying that he was concerned enough to visit me, even though I was no longer one of his charges, nor had I been for many months. I thought it was courageous for him to come to the hospital, since he probably assumed I had learned what happened between him and my father.

Before we could even begin a conversation, before I could tell him how good it made me feel that he came to the hospital to see me, my father "arrived." I was so uncomfortable I wished I were under general anesthesia again.

The coach left after only a few minutes, during which he and my father said nothing to each other, nor do I remember their even looking at each other. The three of us said little at all during this awkward visit.

I knew I'd recover, for the most part, from the knee surgery, but I was much less certain about recovering from my coach's betrayal, even though I could not jettison my fond feelings for him that had evolved over several years. As disheartening as it was, his behavior when I was injured offered me an even deeper appreciation that Miss Dyer had eased me onto *terra firma*. A compassionate French teacher, who had shown no interest in athletics, was the one who encouraged me—and, in my despair and confusion, gave me permission—to choose a new arena, where I no longer would have to ask what books would I read.

Fall 2010. Before driving to St. Louis for my fifty-year high school reunion, I visited my scuffed and dusty high school football shoes hanging from a hook on the wall in the garage. Their once-white laces were an unwashed gray, and the once-shiny aluminum tips of their cleats were dull and worn. I have never been able to leave behind these old friends, and I wanted the memory of them to accompany me on the drive to the reunion.

Somewhere along the four-hundred-mile route, I thought about the old feelings of being somehow "less than" so many of my classmates, about the old refrain, "But, what books will I read?" and about Rolf's question at the dinner table. He wouldn't be at the reunion, having been part of the class a year ahead of me, but I fantasized about seeing him there, anyway.

He seems pleased that I hadn't become an "athletic coach," but had become an anthropologist and attorney. I ask if he'd achieved his professional aspirations, and his answer is yes. This time, I don't feel "less than." It surprises me when he says, "You didn't know I admired that you wanted to be a coach, yes? I was a really good football player, you know, soccer player, and for a long time, I wanted to be a coach. I've always wondered what my life would be if I had followed my heart. Do you ever wonder that?

At a house party one evening during the reunion, I sat at a table with four or five classmates, including Carol. One by one, the other people who sat with us did what I hoped they would do: drift away so she and I could be alone. I moved my chair closer to hers. Fifty years earlier, we'd performed together in Arthur Miller's *All My Sons*. She was a perfect "Mother," Kate Keller, my wife; her performance helped me be a more convincing Joe Keller than I otherwise would have been.

Whenever I think of what happened next in our conversation, I replay it in my mind as if it were a dramatic scene on the stage we had shared so many years earlier.

[The sounds and the auditorium lights fade. The setting is a backyard porch on a summer night. Carol, playing Kate, and Myles, playing Joe, sit alone in a circle of intimacy from the beam of a single spotlight on an otherwise darkened stage. Joe starts to take Kate's hand, but hesitates and withdraws it.]

Joe: There's something I've wanted to tell you for the past fifty years.

Kate: Will I want to hear it? [She says this in her gentle, soft voice. She smiles and tilts her head, looking shy, even a bit self-effacing.]

Joe: I'm sure you'll want to hear it. You know I'd hurt my knee and dropped all the athletics, right?

Kate: Yes, I do know.

Joe: My guess is that you didn't know how much I admired you. You were a great student, and I wanted to be like you. Really, it's kind of simple. I just wanted to be your friend. I didn't think you'd want to be *mine*.

Kate: Joe, you don't . . .

[Joe leans toward her and takes both her hands in his.]

Joe: I couldn't believe we actually became friends. That you wanted to be my friend. I bet you never imagined how much that meant to me.

Kate: Actually, it was the other way around. You were popular, you had a lot of friends . . . I simply couldn't imagine you'd ever consider me one of them. When you paid attention to me, it was wonnnnderful. You accepted me for who I was.

[Joe pauses to contemplate what he just heard; he looks down, then up at her.]

Joe: Do you think this is as amazing as I do?

Kate: Yes. I do. [She nods several times.]

[Joe shifts in his chair slightly toward the audience and delivers his soliloquy.]

Joe: So this is how I figure it. Here sit Kate and Joe, two peas at the far ends of the same pod. And they needed nothing more than a mere half-century to know it.

[They rise and stand in the circle from the beam of the spotlight. Kate gives another of her smiles and seems delighted, as does Joe. Each takes a short step toward each other, and they linger in an enveloping embrace as the spotlight fades, the house lights rise, and a curtain of sounds from the celebration of a fifty-year reunion descends.]

PART III

Surviving Unemployment

Unemployment is capitalism's way of getting you to plant a garden.
—Orson Scott Card, Homebody

THE FORTUNE COOKIE

We haven't seen each other for more than a year, so when we meet for lunch at a Chinese restaurant, we go straight for the hug, then a table, then the buffet.

My lunch companion and I had worked together in a start-up business, but a couple of years ago had gone our separate ways. After a few minutes of "How're the kids" and "How's your wife," for the next two hours, we share our aspirations and fears about being in our seventies and continuing to support our families.

As our plates empty for the second time, I say to him, "I've always admired how you stay involved with different groups and promote your consulting business."

"All I do is put myself out there and see where it leads," he says.

"I worry much more about where it will lead before I put myself out there."

The waiter comes to the table with the customary black plastic tray with two cellophane-wrapped fortune cookies resting on top of the check.

"Those cookies are waiting for us to open them," my friend says.

"I don't think I'll open mine." Uncertain, even

pessimistic, about the future, I can't imagine that a cookie fortune could be anything but disappointing. It's bad enough to be attributing prophetic powers to an inanimate concoction of sugar and flour and a slip of paper.

After giving me one of those "Whatever" stares, complete with a shrug of the shoulders, he opens his cookie, pulls the paper from the half it was hanging out of, and reads it to himself. Smiling, he unbuttons his left shirt pocket and puts the little slip of a fortune safe inside.

"Go ahead and open yours," he says, patting his pocket. "They're never bad."

"What the hell. All right." It's easier to open the cookie than to argue with him about it.

I pick up the cookie and just stare at it. An unpleasant memory from a few years earlier returns, a warning of sorts. I'm in a hotel room trying hard to tear open a cellophane-wrapped bar of soap. After repeated failures, and eschewing the use of my little travel scissors, I think it's a good idea to adopt a traditional practice—sometimes employed by Inuit and other women—of softening animal hides by chewing on them. In the event, I suffer no more than a broken front tooth and an hour of frantic calls until finding a dentist to perform a temporary repair before my lunch meeting, at which I settle for a bowl of broth and extra napkins, which catch what dribbles down my chin.

This time, the cellophane tears easily between my fingers. I crack open the pale yellow crescent and cup both halves in my hands.

"Why did I open this goddamn thing?"

"What's it say?"

"Nothing."

"They always say *something*."

I hand him the halves, which he inspects like a gemologist using a loupe.

"It's empty," he says.

"Yes. I know."

He hands the pieces back to me and, like the cookie itself, says nothing more. I remember with irritation that he often keeps his thoughts to himself, when it would help if he didn't. We stand up to leave, and while I put the cash and tip on the plastic tray, we do laugh a little about what happened.

Outside, we shake hands, promise to meet again "soon," agree that it's his turn to pay for the next lunch, and walk in opposite directions toward our cars. I step from the curb into a puddle of slush, which soaks my shoe and sock. I swear out loud at that misfortune, but at least when I turn the key in my car door lock, it unlocks, and when I turn the key in the ignition, the engine starts.

Before I pull into traffic, I take a moment to think of those millions of cellophane-wrapped, crescent cookies that are unwrapped and broken open every day around the world. One of them contains what was supposed to have been my fortune, but now is destined for some other lucky soul: *Much success on road in front, but taking great care where stepping.*

Mindful of the fortune that should have been mine, I drive with great care, obey the speed limit, make complete stops, and ignore the other drivers who blast their horns. If I didn't know better, I'd think they're waving hello as they pass. I'm not sure why they look so angry.

ROBIN HOOD IN THE COFFEE OFFICE

A Letter to an Anthropologist Colleague and Friend

January 7, 2013

Dear Mike,

This letter is long overdue, but I'm glad I waited until now to write. I'm pretty sure today is about a month past the forty-fourth anniversary of our occupation and liberation.

I've been reminiscing (with myself) about how you inched your way along the second floor ledge of MacMillan Hall and climbed through what's-his-name's office window so we could liberate his furniture and use it for "our new office." Remember I was afraid of heights, and you said I should just stand below the ledge and try to catch you in case you fell? Thank God you didn't.

About that new office of ours: What choice did we two grad students have? There was no furniture, and we needed some, right? By the way, did we ever find out who was supposed to occupy that office? Didn't Annie tell us who it was? All I remember is she said he was really pissed off, and he was in the chairman's office trying to get him to evict us.

Well, in honor of the anniversary, I'm working here

on the same kind of thing, this time with the head of maintenance. I have my eye on a sink and cabinet that look . . . Wait. I'm sorry. I'm getting way ahead of the story. Let me back up a bit.

To begin with, I'm seventy years old (by the way, it's my birthday—no gifts, please), and I still make a few questionable decisions. I should have turned down the offer to direct the ex-offender program. In any event, I'll be leaving here soon, even though what we're doing is important. We do help our clients find employment, but the physical and social environment here is toxic. You and I should be studying this place, instead of my working here.

Our offices are in the lower level of a three-story building. Some of the people in the "upper levels" refer to ours as the "basement" (and sometimes sniff when they say it), even though there are large windows above the grade of the sidewalk. Go figure.

How many cups of coffee have we enjoyed together over close to fifty years? Thousands? You might think having good coffee where I work would be a simple matter in 2013, but you'd be wrong. The employees from another program located near mine have the use of a small room they refer to as "the kitchen," though it has no running water, and two old dormitory refrigerators to serve the needs of a dozen people. The microwave is so worn out you have to select two minutes to heat something the equivalent of thirty seconds; the coffeepot sounds like a lawn mower; the coffee itself is horrible; the cups are an almost gossamer-thin Styrofoam; utensils are disposable plastic that should have been disposed of at the factory; and if you hold a full paper plate by anything but the bottom, it droops as if it had melted. If you bring a cup or plate from home, the only place to wash it is a bathroom used by staff, visitors, and clients. Unpleasant.

Here's something to agitate your anti-capitalist soul: The poorly paid, underappreciated "basement" employees, including my own staff and me, are provided nothing in the way of coffee, tea, and other refreshments by an agency with an annual budget of more than $20,000,000. Yes, you read that correctly. The subversive part of your soul will be pleased when I share with you the conversation I initiated with the associate director, whose office is on the upper level. I mean, where else would it be? I wish I could tell you I'm joking, Mike, but this is how it unfolded. I remember most of it almost word for word.

> Me: I'm about to use my budget to buy coffee for my staff and anyone else from other programs who helps us.
> Charles: You know we have to be careful how we spend our money.
> Me: Are you aware that Thomas personally pays for the coffee and supplies for everyone on his team, and then invites *my* team to help ourselves? I have a high salary, Charles, but no one else downstairs does, and the working conditions are horrible. It's not acceptable to ignore this.

I thought he might capitulate, but instead . . .

Charles: I didn't know about Thomas. Can't he ask everyone to chip in?
(Yep . . . he said, *chip in*.)
Me: If they could afford to chip in, Charles, they already would have.
Charles: You're probably right, but what if *everyone* in the agency wants free coffee?
Me: If you provide it to *everyone*, you'll have several hundred people with higher morale, not to mention more money in their pockets.
Charles: But, consider that not everyone drinks *coffee. Then* what?

You probably think I'm making some of this up, but I actually had to say he could pay for tea and hot chocolate along with the coffee. I'm sure you already know his response.

Charles: That could work if everyone chipped in a few dollars a week.
Me: You don't ask that of the high-salaried people on this floor.
Charles: Well, you're probably right, again. That does seem unfair, doesn't it? What if people come up to the second floor and make their drinks? Then you wouldn't have to spend money on coffee machines and all of the supplies.
Me: Charles . . . please. You're saying that someone should wait downstairs for the slowest elevator in North America, make a drink in your kitchen, and walk back with it to the same elevator? When

a *group* of people want coffee, should *all* of them
make this trek? By the time they got back to our
offices downstairs, they wouldn't even remember
why they were there . . . and they'd be drinking
coffee that was already cold.

So, he then says that a "good solution" would be if
someone comes to the second floor and makes coffee in
one of the thermos dispensers and brings it downstairs. He
said the agency's budget would pay for the thermoses, and
everyone downstairs can chip in (yep, again) some money
every week. I just stared and kind of shook my head because
this conversation was certifiably bonkers—but not unusual
for this place.

Charles: Wouldn't the thermoses solve the
problem?
Me: Not unless you pay for *everything*, not just
the thermoses. Forgive me, but you're saying the
same thing over and over, Charles. I give up. Let's
just forget about all this.
Charles: That's best for now.

A friend of mine is responsible for maintaining the
equipment in the buildings this agency owns or rents. I
asked him if any refrigerators were being replaced, and, if
so, would he give us the best one that's on its way out. The
next day, his guys moved a used, attractive refrigerator into
"the kitchen," and moved the two dormitory refrigerators,
one to a storage room, and the other to my office. Two days

later, his guys showed up with an almost new microwave oven and a Mr. Coffee machine. I gave Thomas some of my own money for supplies for *his* team, to repay him for having been so generous to *my* team.

Now, on my frequent (and sometimes necessary) visits to the upper level, I operate in Robin Hood mode. All I'm missing is the rest of the Band of Merry Men to participate in liberating packets of hot chocolate, tea bags, sugar, creamer, and a few other things, like sturdy plastic utensils, instant soup, and oatmeal—but not the brewed coffee. It's too damn weak to drink, and half of it is flavored. Flavored! Like French Vanilla, Hazelnut Creme, Mocha-something-or-other, Decaf Linzertorte, and others that are unspeakable. Do Norwegians even drink this stuff?

But something kind of wonderful did happen, Mike. Not long after the redistribution of wealth (your Scandinavian socialist soul must be rejoicing), my administrative assistant brought in a Keurig coffee maker. She had it at home, said she never used it, and knew I'd enjoy the coffee. She also brought a rotating "tower" with pod holders on both sides. We keep the equipment in her office, which is much bigger than mine. She needs the room; I don't.

I do everything I can to help her advance. This agency is supposed to help ex-offenders find employment, but I had to persuade them to hire her. Why did I have to persuade them? She'd have to deal with the petty cash box, they said, and that *concerned* them, they added. You guessed it: because she is an ex-offender! By the way, there's only about fifteen bucks in the box at any time, not to mention that her prior offense had been totally unrelated to theft of any kind.

If you haven't been with a Keurig, Mike, you're missing something. She makes me happy when I hear her soft murmuring, the sound of water and steam being forced through the pod, and the stream of coffee filling the cup. Oh, I forgot to mention that I also take some nice, heavy-duty Styrofoam cups from upstairs, and they fit her perfectly. God knows, I've grown to love Mademoiselle Keurig. I stand in front of her while she fills my cup, and she winks at me with her little blue eye. She reminds me of a female R2-D2. Same tribal clan, you think?

When people around the agency learned that Keurig had joined us, they started to visit our offices. Some arrived agitated, or just plain lonely. It's like they come for a bit of informal talk, kind of like informal therapy. Madame Doctor Keurig is an R2-D2 of a therapist with unlimited office hours, walk-ins welcome.

It's interesting how Keurig and I coordinate. For example, a guy I really like comes to the office almost every day and heads straight for Keurig. He just smiles at her as she makes his drink, and then he turns and starts talking to *me*. Earlier today, he launched into lengthy reportage about what his supervisor had done to him that morning.

For fifteen minutes, all he heard from me was one "Let's just sit and relax," a few "I understand how you feel," a couple "Please, go on," and—you'll be impressed—only *one* "You're *serious*? He actually *said* that?" (I have an excuse for my transgression: He was talking about the associate director I wanted to defenestrate a week or so earlier during our conversation about who pays for coffee.) By the end of our time together, he was able to laugh at himself. When I said, "I have to get back to work now" (which might have sounded like, "It's time to stop for today"), he said, "Hey—my wife and I are going shopping this weekend. I'll bring in a box of pods on Monday. I really like this Keurig."

Now we have a different problem. He brought a couple boxes of coffee pods and cider pods (apple with cinnamon; not bad, but kind of sweet) that we added to our own ample supply that includes two plastic grocery bags overflowing with dozens of hot chocolate pods that another colleague was given by someone at the hospital where he moonlights. We're swamped with pods, but we can't refuse our visitors' offerings, and there's no way we can cut our open office hours. That wouldn't be fair, would it?

Yesterday, I realized something else that's important about Keurig. She's versatile. Not only does she appear to be trained in psychotherapy, she also seems to be proficient in what I call (with apologies to Dr. Freud) "Pyroanalysis." Keurig is, after all, quite a bit like a fireplace. Without having to say a word, and in a blink of her beautiful blue eye, she turns our office into a warm hearth, where visitors find refuge from the cold, dark realities of their work.

Before you call Catherine to ask if she thinks I'm okay, I'll tell you the last part of this tale. Those sorry laborers on the "upper level" drink coffee brewed by a guy named Bunn. He's no R2-D2, that's for sure. He's built like a stainless steel box with little plastic appendages, and has an awful personality, flat affect, and no alluring voice. As for the lovely blue eye that winks like Keurig's does when she's pleased? Forget about it!

I feel sorry for the poor guy. I mean, he's attached to a

stainless steel supply line, as if he's on life support. Worse yet, I never see anyone linger with Bunn. Everyone gets out of his way quickly, like when people visit someone in the hospital who's really sick and might not make it.

Anyway, those upper-level people don't have a clue. They seem unable to understand what we have in our basement and how much they're missing. I mean, even if they don't care about providing a fireplace and warm hearth, for God's sake, can't they understand that kids need a safe clubhouse where their parents can't drive them crazy?

That's about it for now, dear friend. I wish I'd listened to your advice way back in 1980, when I decided to work in my family's business. All I can say is, at least where I am now is *supposed* to be nonprofit.

I definitely must get out of this basement.

As always, love from Catherine and me,

Myles

THE RETAINING WALL

When more and more people are thrown out of work,
unemployment results.
—Calvin Coolidge

Summer 2014. With the customary warmth befitting state government, the letter contained thoughtful reminders concerning the orientation required of anyone seeking unemployment compensation: "Attendance is mandatory . . . If you fail . . . You must bring . . ."

These instructions made me as angry as when I read the impenetrable language of job postings. Right before the full-afternoon orientation session, in an inexplicable act of masochism, I read again the page of excerpts from postings I had collected and intended to bring with me. Just looking at the page of paper reminded me why I was well-served by daily meditation, some good whiskey, and occasional prayer.

My plan was to read these three postings, so the people in charge of today's picnic were going to learn I was onto their game and the charade they were making us attend.

. . . The Organization and Position Specialist is a new role within a new function created to broaden new Service

Delivery services and to provide high touch service to Managers to reduce the complexity associated with position management and complex job changes. This team will create positive manager experience with regards to position management . . . This role will play an integral role in the manager experience and have a critical impact on Managers . . .

"You didn't understand?" I planned to say to the unemployment officials squirming in their office chairs. "Let's try the next one. It'll be easier for you."

. . . BASIC FUNCTION: Enhances field productivity, efficiency and profitability through Financial Representative facing consultation to best practices, benchmarks, tools and resources that help financial representatives manage their practice as an entrepreneur. Desirable qualifications: Experience with practice management philosophies/ programs. Experience with practice management philosophies/programs [*sic*].

"Laugh all you want," I planned to say. "Here comes the only one you'll understand."

. . . Demonstrates a commitment to and proficiency in the engagement of non-evaluation and non-researchers in the evaluation and research process . . . Qualifications: Personal experience with mental illness is a prerequisite for this position.

In spite of being beyond agitated, and about to change my clothes and go work in the garden, I decided to drive to the appointment *not* armed with the printed sheet of job postings. I arrived ten minutes early, parked on the street, and sat in the car. Fifty feet in front of me, a small grocery and variety store anchored the corner of the intersection. Where the sidewalk met the lawn of the house adjacent to the store, a man sat on a low concrete retaining wall. Immobile, his head bowed, he seemed to be staring at something at his feet.

It's a total snafu for you, isn't it? You must have just left the unemployment office, and I'm going to be taking your place.

I walked to a building that had the look of a detention center. In the foyer, an armed security guard said the room I wanted was right down the hall. Bewildered as to why there were two lines in the room instead of one, I chose the line nearer the door. In a few minutes, I stood before the receptionist, sixty-something years old, who sat at her low desk behind a tall counter, requiring each person to look down at her while she often did not look up.

With a friendly "Hello," I handed her my letter.

She gave it a quick scan, looked up at me, and said, "Get in behind those people," pointing to the second line three feet away from us.

In two minutes, I stood before another official, in his late forties, positioned upright and within arm's reach of the receptionist's counter. "Please tell me my papers are okay," I said, a smile pasted onto my face. Out of fear that I might be sent home and have to return another day, I had placed all of my documents in separate and labeled file folders to make it easier on anyone who might ask for them.

"Lemme see your papers," he said.

I have to get out of here. What if this guy sends me back to the first line, the receptionist sends me to this line again, and I go back and forth like a goddamn idiot all day? What am I, a Roomba vacuum cleaner? Hit a wall, turn around, hit a wall across the room, keep going until there's nothing left in its electric heart. No wonder that guy was sitting immobilized on the retaining wall.

"Let's see here . . . yep, you've done that . . . okay . . . yep. It's all here. Have a seat at a table over there until we're ready."

I sat with two women. At the table next to us, two men, who also had run the gauntlet and survived, were in a conversation. Within a few more minutes, the three tables had filled with four men and six women. The official of the second line walked over to our tables and said, "Okay, everyone. Follow me. It's a long walk." It might have been the result of having experienced two unemployment office lines that we followed him in what would best be described as a clump. He led us to a windowless room, about twenty by twenty feet, suffused with cold fluorescent light . . . the kind that makes it fun to work in an office. Six tables with steel legs and off-white laminated tops had been arranged in a U-shape. The ingenious, flexible backs of the steel-legged, blue plastic chairs allowed sitters to recline as much as fifteen degrees, thus relieving pressure on the coccyx and guaranteeing that at least something here won't be a total pain in the ass.

At the opening of the U, a wheeled cart held a laptop connected to a projector pointed at a screen, all of which indicated we soon would be rewarded with the dreaded PowerPoint. The leader took his place next to the cart and said, "I shouldn't be here today. The person who does this orientation doesn't feel good, so I'm filling in. Let's start by going around the room. Only your first names, and your last job."

A woman, two to my left, began the exercise the right way. The woman next to me messed up, and I mean royally, by stating her last name. The leader reminded us to be careful, looked at me, and said, "You're up."

I wasn't just careful; I was *extra* careful. "My name is Myles. M-y-l-e-s." I was aware that I was being provocative. It bothered me, but I wouldn't stop.

"What's the 'l-e-s' all about? I don't understand," the leader said.

"It's not 'l-e-s,' it's *M-y*-l-e-s. A lot of people spell it with an 'i.'"

"Oh." He shrugged his shoulders.

"Your last job?" the leader reminded me.

"I developed and directed an employment program for ex-offenders. But the program ended, and I would like the unemployment compensation."

"Then you could be doing *my* job," he said.

"I guess so, but then *you* wouldn't be doing it."

"And that's why *you're* not going to be doing it," he said, ending this transaction.

I berated myself for talking to him the way I did. I deserved his response, and I was embarrassed.

After the rest of the group used first names only when completing the exercise, the leader opened the laptop to display the first page of his PowerPoint. "Okay. We have much to cover. So, what do you do if you think your résumé is not helping?" Slight pause. "You immediately prepare a better one. It's the most important document. I can use a résumé that says I'm a welder, which I am. But what does that tell the employer? But what if I write that I'm a welder, and list the materials I weld, and my industry certifications? Which is better?" Slight pause. "It's obvious, right? I've had to do this myself at least eight times in my career. I really feel for what all of you are going through."

Hey. I kinda like this guy . . . unpretentious, trying to help . . . look at everyone taking notes . . . small business owner, executives, administrative assistants, health care aides, computer whiz . . . and M-y-l-e-s, at least twenty years older than the next oldest person here, now letting go of the anger and defensiveness from earlier in the day.

Another hour of lecture and PowerPoint on résumé preparation, interviewing, and job search websites had passed, and I had begun to feel connected with the others at the table. I had walked through a door into a space I never anticipated I would be in, and there was something I liked about it. I even was taking notes in the margins of the handouts. As we neared the end of the session, I took full advantage of the flexible feature of my chair as I leaned back and let my thoughts wander.

I'll write about this day, about that attitude I arrived with. My struggle is no worse than his, or hers, or anyone else's here. If the PowerPoint were a book, hundreds, thousands of the hopeful and despondent who have sat in this room would have stained its yellowed and dog-eared pages with drops of coffee, and more than a few tears. That executive across from me. Taking pages of notes. Early fifties. White shirt and tie. Kids in college? Broke? The two young women next to me? Going where? For what? To wind up working in a dead end?

"...finished, and we covered a lot," the leader concluded. "Take the brochures, go online, read your notes, don't give up. Now, you'll meet one-on-one with counselors to see if you're on the right track with your résumés, cover letters, and job search. When I call your name, or someone else comes to the room and does, we'll tell you who you meet with. I'll meet with the first person." He called the first name and escorted a woman into a small office attached to the conference room.

After half an hour, when only one woman and I remained at the table, an official came to the door and said I should follow her down the hall. "Here you are," she said motioning to an open door. I stepped into a mid-size conference room; having sat under nothing but artificial lighting for the last two hours, the natural light from a wall of windows felt restorative. At a corner of the closed square of tables—same off-white, same blue chairs—a slim manila folder rested in front of my counselor, a man in his late thirties, early forties. He didn't greet me; he didn't say anything at all, nor did he get up from where he was sitting at the table.

"Hi. I'm Myles." He didn't respond, but did grimace and shift in his chair. "But you know that, right?"

"Sure. Sit down." He gestured to the chair on the other side of the corner of the table. I sat, he shifted again in his chair, grimaced, pushed the file toward me, didn't introduce himself, and said, "This is yours."

It was obvious that he wasn't well, and that gave me a clue about him. "Are you the person who was supposed to lead our group, instead of the person who said he shouldn't be here today?"

"Yeah, I am. I have a back problem. I've been taking pain pills, and they help a little."

"Oh . . . I've had back surgery and took that kind of pill. Are you sure we should be having this counseling session? It's okay with me if we skip it."

"I'm okay." Another shift and grimace. "But, I don't see how I can help you. You have all this experience, a PhD, law degree, all the rest."

Wondering, then, why in the world I was required to be here, I glanced at the name on his business card clipped to my file. "Is your background Hungarian?"

"No. I'm a Gypsy."

"Romanian? Near Hungary? Have you read *King of the Gypsies* by Peter Mass?"

"No, I haven't. A long time ago, our family was in Ireland. You know . . . Black Irish, but I only visited once, when I was stationed in Europe."

"What branch of the service were you in?" I said.

"Air Force. Special Ops. I can't tell you much, but we were ahead of the other troops."

"What'd you do?"

"I was a good shot," he said.

"You were a sniper?"

"Let's just say I didn't miss many shots." He smiled.

It seemed like a good moment for me to say, "Since you're my counselor, I guess you need to know what I want to do."

"You're right. What *do* you want to do?" He shifted in his chair and grimaced, yet again.

"I love to write, and that's what I want to do. If I must have a job, I'd prefer to do what *you* do." Feeling charitable, I had refrained from, "I want to use my broad and deep skills and experience to help an organization fulfill its mission and vision." Consuming that sort of horrendous drivel, after he'd consumed some powerful pain pills, would have rendered him unconscious, if not deceased.

"I like to write, too," my counselor said. "I wanted to be a teacher, like you were. I was in a PhD program in creative writing. They liked my proposal for a novel I had started. I was illustrating it with my photographs. I'm a photographer. At the last minute, they decided I couldn't do it. No good explanation."

"So, instead, you work here full time. Will you have to stay for many more years?"

"With my wife's and my pensions, we don't worry. I can take mine in a few years."

"My career advice is stay put." With a smooth shifting of gears that would have impressed no less than Mario Andretti, I said, "But, it's pretty clear you can't help me, right?"

"I'm sorry. You know you might have to take something you're way too qualified to do."

After we reviewed the errors to avoid when completing mandatory, weekly job search reports, I pushed away from the table and said, "Thank you for your time."

He remained seated, in obvious discomfort. "No problem. Call or email anytime you want to talk or you have questions. That counts as one of your job searches."

"That's a surprise. Do I understand you correctly that our required number of job searches can include a phone conversation with you? And all I'd have to do is ask something like, 'What do you think about this job I ran across?'"

"Yes, I suppose so."

"Well, thank you for the time you've given me today. Would you like me to close the door as I leave?"

"No, that's okay. You can leave the door open."

I wanted to say that I always do, but what would the point have been?

Like an actor in a film running in reverse, I retraced my steps up the hall, out the front door, and into my car. I made a Y-turn, but before driving away, I checked the rearview mirror. I expected to see my buddy sitting on the concrete retaining wall, and I was disappointed that he wasn't there.

AN UNEXPECTED INTIMACY

Wisconsin winter, 2010. Late afternoon. The living room and my mood are the color of gloom. I'm alone, and when the doorbell rings, I'm certain it will be another "Can you help with our church?" or another "We can fix your siding. Cheap." I decide that I needn't answer the door or the telephone, should it ring. I can even keep the lights off, if I so choose, which I do.

I stand up and look through the sheer curtains. A lamppost flickers twice, then stays on, and a UPS driver climbs into his truck and drives away. Thinking he must have been the one who rang the doorbell, I open the door and recover a box I forgot I had ordered.

The coming spring will be our first in a rental house that has no gardens, only neglected beds. In response to a drastic, unexpected series of events, Catherine and I closed the sale of our home two months earlier. We had hoped our yet unborn grandchildren might visit us there; we would help them learn the names of all the plants in the gardens which had given our family the prior nine and a half years of happiness, and a sense of permanence. This sorrow was not without company. Immediately after the closing, Catherine listened on her phone to the voicemail one of her siblings had left. During the closing, their terminally ill father had slipped into a coma. He would die the next morning. Our nineteen-year-old daughter and twenty-one-year-old son came home from college for the funeral, which was when they first saw the house we rented, intending to stay for a one-year transition, and still rent ten years later.

I return to the rocking chair, switch on the table lamp, and open the box from UPS containing everything necessary for an indoor hydroponic garden. I ordered this hoping it might help me fight my despondency, which was sure to last through the winter, if not longer.

Sleet taps on the window. In the warm room, I feel cold and begin to think *coffee*. But the idea of drinking it here, alone, isn't a good one, so I drive to the local café. The barista wears her dark brown hair in a ponytail, which I like. When she asks customers what she can get for them, her hazel eyes are big and round. I place my order, and she says she'll bring it to me.

The only other customer is immersed in her book and doesn't look at me when I sit down at the table across the room from her. We're in *Nighthawks*, the Hopper painting of the late night patrons sitting alone, together, in the diner.

In the corner between us, the flames of a gas fireplace dance a blue, yellow, and red-orange jitterbug. Outside, everything is a wet, metallic gray. The coffee grinder grinds coffee, the steam wand begins to steam, and I inhale the aroma of freshly ground Italian Roast with notes of chocolate and spice.

The barista approaches and places a *cappuccino* on the table. In this place, no one snickers when a customer orders a *cappuccino* in the afternoon. I examine her artistry—a perfect, white foam flower that graces the surface of the espresso. I nestle the white ceramic cup in both hands, like I would the root ball of a plant ready for its place in the ground, and remember that my wife had told me that when our daughter was a little girl, she said, "If I'm walking home, I know I'm there when I can see Daddy's flowers."

I close my eyes, and a scene from the coming spring takes shape.

The single father who bought our home, the one with "Daddy's flowers," begins to stroll with his infant daughter in the dappled sunlight of the gardens we left behind. The season of spring ephemerals will last for weeks; but, in this scene, the season is compressed into no more than a few moments. The father carries her out of and then into sunlight, and the curls of her blonde hair flash golden. Their first steps take them past daffodils and hyacinths, Solomon's seal, Jacob's ladder, and mayapples. They stroll farther down the wood chip path and pause to admire English bluebells and lady's slippers. They continue to walk past bleeding hearts, columbines, and trilliums, white and pink. As they reach the side yard, he points to a bed of Grecian windflowers and drifts of sweet woodruff coated with a foam of tiny, white flowers. As the path turns, they walk among lilies of the valley, snowdrops, and crocuses. He points to a bed of tulips, red and yellow. Father and daughter continue toward the front of the house, but I leave them.

The flames in the fireplace now do a slow dance, and my body relaxes in a way it hasn't in months. I'm relieved to have taken such pleasure in the images of father and daughter discovering the wondrous floral array that now is theirs.

The pattern of drops on the outside of the café window says the sleet has stopped, and what falls is only a light, cold rain. I sit for a while and finish my coffee, while the barista is in the back room and the other customer is immersed in her book. I wonder if she's familiar with *Nighthawks*.

I put on my jacket and walk to the car. Driving home, I fixate on the windshield wipers that move and sound like the metronome that rested on our chestnut-colored baby grand piano.

We inherit the piano from dear friends of my deceased parents . . . our children are little and begin lessons . . . our daughter says to me, "Daddy, listen to me play 'Twinkle, Twinkle Little Star'" . . . she does . . . she says she can play it backwards . . . she does . . . swivels on the bench and her back is toward the keyboard . . . raises her arms above her head, and plays the song again . . . we sell the piano to a couple who say they are pleased that their children will learn to play on such a wonderful instrument . . . the movers arrive and dismember our precious possession, place the legs on one cart and the body on another . . . they roll the carts to their truck, parked outside like a waiting ambulance, then leave with our piano.

I pull the car into the driveway and sit for a few minutes, surprised that I find solace in the thought that there is a young family living in a home that once was ours, and another young family playing a baby grand that once was ours. It feels like we share with each of these families an unexpected intimacy.

The rain is only a light drizzle when I leave the car and walk to the backyard. It's dark, but I begin bringing the gardening tools from the wooden shed into the garage. There, in comparative warmth, October's dirt can be cleaned from the spades and hand tools in anticipation of spring planting, after what promises to be a long winter. I haven't decided where to store all the tools and supplies, and this simple task threatens to become overwhelming.

I begin to feel better when I remember what our new neighbor, Frank, said to me after we moved into our home. "I know your garden will be beautiful. You'd been here only a week or so, and on a cold night in mid-October I looked outside, and there you were in the moonlight, tilling the soil."

PART IV

The Other

. . .We love and lose in China,
we weep on England's moors,
and laugh and moan in Guinea,
and thrive on Spanish shores.

We seek success in Finland,
are born and die in Maine.
In minor ways we differ,
in major we're the same.

I note the obvious differences
between each sort and type,
but we are more alike, my friends,
than we are unalike.

We are more alike, my friends,
than we are unalike.

We are more alike, my friends,
than we are unalike.

—Maya Angelou, "Human Family"

LEO'S GIFT

The simplest acts of kindness are by far more powerful
than a thousand heads bowing in prayer.
—Mahatma Gandhi

At age fifteen, I learned something important from a person I had assumed was the least likely to teach me anything. It was summer, 1958, and I was working in my parents' small, retail fur garment business in the old commercial district of downtown St. Louis.

Around that same time, they had declared bankruptcy. I didn't know much about bankruptcy except it wasn't a good thing to declare. I also didn't know that it had happened to my father and mother and their children. My parents didn't tell us, at least not me. They were silent and ashamed.

I first became aware of it when I was in the locker room getting dressed for a high school baseball game. "I heard your parents went bankrupt," one of my teammates said as we sat side by side on the bench in front of our lockers. "My parents told me they read about it."

"Oh . . . yeah . . . I know. Well, I guess it happens. No big deal," I said, unable to look at him.

With ninety dollars I had earned from part-time work

at my parents' store, I bought a 1949 four-door Plymouth from a friend of my father. I didn't have a driver's license yet, but both men assured me it was a smart buy, and I'd need it within the year, anyway. I gave it to my parents, since they had just lost theirs in the bankruptcy proceedings. I also gave them whatever other money I had left in my meager savings account—about one hundred dollars.

I was with them in that dingy Plymouth, with its shredded and missing upholstery on the doors, when we drove by someone we knew. My mother said to my father, "There's Mrs. Peters," but neither of them turned to wave. I looked in Mrs. Peters's direction only by moving my eyes far to the right.

My parents recovered from bankruptcy and rebuilt their business. They were kind people who had little money, but shared it with others; in the future, when they had more, they shared more. They believed this was the right thing, the kind thing, to do. Another way they expressed their kindness and social concern during all their years in business was by hiring a diverse workforce of part-time, full-time, and whenever-there's-something-to-do employees, a few of whom might otherwise have been unemployable. They hired women, men, Jews, Christians, Muslims, blacks, whites, young and old, with a variety of sexual orientations and gender identities. And this was years before "diversity in the workplace" would be accepted and expected, especially in a near-Southern city like St. Louis.

By any standard, this workforce was composed of an extraordinary array of uncommon people. A mild-mannered, vulnerable young man in his early thirties sported a flamboyant wardrobe and a shiny bouffant hairdo always set to perfection. Another man in his early twenties often appeared in a suit and tie and carried a couple of sociology books to convey the impression he was a college student, although he told my father that he never had learned to read. He said he wanted to create "a professional appearance." There was a man in his sixties who had been declared "legally blind," an inconvenience that didn't stop him from driving to and from work, or anywhere else, in his four-door Buick.

A favorite of mine was "Beans," a traveling salesman in his thirties who regaled me with fanciful stories of his many adventures, one of which he said had taken place in high school. In front of a large crowd, he decided to jump over a low, wooden barrier on the sidelines in order to race onto the field as a substitute during a football game. Unfortunately, he succeeded only in knocking himself unconscious when his hand slipped off the top railing. Somehow, in that same story, he managed to find a way to tell me that in high school, and for some years beyond, his daily breakfast consisted of a kosher pickle and a Pepsi. I loved his stories, and never believed any of them. Not a word.

In addition to those employees who were flamboyant, self-absorbed, or dissembling, there were others who were quiet, sometimes self-effacing, but always exemplars of honesty and trustworthiness. Their contributions might have seemed small to those who didn't know better, but they never failed to repay loyalty with loyalty. They helped the business thrive, and the business did the same for them. If these gentle souls—I will not call them meek—might not inherit the Earth, at least they will have made it worth inhabiting.

The dearest of these people was Lilly, a seamstress in her thirties. Lilly was like a member of the family, often in our home to visit and share a meal. She would smile, and hug, and love and be loved. There were times when the business struggled to meet its payroll, and Lilly would offer, without having been asked, to postpone her pay.

And there was Dave Berger, who came out of retirement to provide needed skills in credit and financial management. His preferred method of locomotion made him seem indefatigable as he leaned forward from the waist, almost trotting from place to place with quick, short steps, holding in both hands a file folder as if it were a serving tray. Because of my parents' affection for him, and his for them, when he asked them to hire his brother, Leo, they did.

Leo had a severe intellectual impairment, but was able to perform tasks that didn't require perfection or completion, such as sweeping floors, moving lightweight objects from one place to another, and helping seal envelopes. I never asked Leo's age, but he seemed to be around fifty years old. He was of medium height and build. His clean, pressed slacks were cinched with a leather belt high on his waist so the pants cuffs never touched his shoes. He wore short-sleeved, light-colored sport shirts that coordinated with his slacks, his hair was always combed, and his shoes were always clean, though not always shined.

In contrast to his older brother's rapid locomotion, Leo moved his feet about twelve inches at a time in a half-walk-half-shuffle and took a long time to get to where he was going. Whether standing still or in motion, he kept both arms straight down, palms facing his legs. His middle fingers twitched toward and away from his palms in rapid repetition.

We would speak only a few words or short sentences to Leo at any one time: "Good morning, Leo," or "How are you today, Leo?" or "Can you help me with this, Leo?" He would answer with only a word or two: "Hello," or "Yes," sometimes "Thank you." He seemed so detached from my reality, and I was so unable to enter his, I can't remember ever trying to have even the simplest conversation with him. I also can't remember ever hearing my parents try.

Summer was the slowest time of the year for our business, so there were days when the only people present were my mother, father, Leo, and I. My own tasks included running errands, helping track inventory, and organizing various business records in the air-conditioned comfort of the front office area and store. Part of every day, I worked in the warmer and stuffier storage and supply rooms in the rear, packing and unpacking boxes of hangers, garments, and pelts, and sweeping the old wooden floor, worn smooth from years of traffic. The dusty wood had a pleasant, almost imperceptible aroma of very lightly-scented talcum powder that, along with the warm air, made it difficult for me to stay awake on those days when I had behaved like a teenager until late the night before.

On most afternoons, I'd take a break and buy cold drinks for us at the nearby Missouri Bar and Grill, a hangout of politicians and police. To get there, I'd walk out the back door and down the ramp to our alley, lined on both sides with loading docks and paved with the original, reddish-brown cobblestones, as were the other alleys in the commercial area of the city. The docks always were filled with interesting people just hanging out while waiting to unload or load trucks, smoking cigarettes during their breaks, and, I imagined, doing all sorts of other things I didn't know much about, but, at my age, would have loved to learn.

In order to reach the cobblestones from the back door of the store, you could use a long, sloping ramp or, if you were sixteen and needed to look cool in front of the older guys hanging out and watching your every move, you could jump off the dock and head for the Bar and Grill. We'd wave hello and give each other a simple "How's it goin'?" and "Not too bad. You?" My wave of choice was to keep my hand at belt height and give a quick side-to-side movement.

It was not uncool to use the ramp on the return trip.

One afternoon, not out of the ordinary, I walked to the Bar and Grill and bought extra-large lemonades "to go, not too much ice, please." Carrying the cardboard drink tray, I entered our back rooms and continued through the swinging door into the air-conditioned front store.

My mother and I enjoyed our drinks in the small, open alcove, which served as an office. My father enjoyed his in another part of the store where he had been taking inventory. In a few minutes, the sound of shuffling feet announced Leo's approach from the back rooms where I hadn't noticed him when I returned with the drinks. Using his shoulder to push open the swinging door, he shuffled into the cool air where my mother and I sat. As always, his middle fingers twitched, but this time he was pale and his breathing was labored. A soft moan accompanied each exhale. He placed his right hand over his heart and made a few more shuffles, twitching only his left middle finger.

"Leo, what's wrong? What is it?" my mother said as we stood and moved toward him.

There was no response save for a twitching finger, a hand over heart, labored breaths, and soft moans on the exhale. We helped him onto the couch where he lay with his torso, left arm, and left leg stretched out on the cushions, his right foot resting on the floor and his head supported by a small pillow.

My mother tried again. "Leo . . . please . . . what can we do to help you?" she implored.

After a pause of a few seconds, Leo said to one or both of us. "Get . . . me . . . a lemonade."

The look on my mother's face said nothing less than, "Thank God, what a relief, I thought he was having a heart attack, but can you *believe* this?"

Had anyone noticed my own look, they would have seen, "This is kind of funny, but it's not . . . and how could I have forgotten Leo?" Seeing that he wasn't dying, and confident that my mother wouldn't need to be revived, I rushed through the back room and down the ramp to the cobblestones and the Bar and Grill, where I ordered a lemonade—the one that would have fit into the empty holder in the four-drink tray I had carried not a half hour earlier.

When I returned, Leo was sitting upright, my mother sitting next to him, and my father standing in front of the couch. Seeing there was no emergency, he returned to his inventory work. I handed Leo his lemonade and said I was sorry to have forgotten to buy him one. He used both hands to hold his drink and sipped it through a straw. When he finished, he rose from the couch without assistance and shuffled through the swinging door.

Sixty years later, I look back, and there's nothing to obscure the view of that day—no veil, no haze of any kind. Even at my young age, I should have understood the value of Leo's gift. In the only way he could, he had communicated his distress: he was one of our group, was someone who mattered, not someone to remain almost unseen and almost unheard.

Yet, "Get me a lemonade" began to be used in banter among my brothers and me to answer variations of "What do you want?" This continued into our adulthoods, although it has diminished to next to never. In those few instances, I've been the one to quote Leo and to imitate how he twitched his fingers. As I recall, our parents never participated in any of this banter. Any humor they might have found in what had occurred with Leo, they kept to themselves, as I wish I had done.

Even now, there are rare moments when I'm tempted to use, "Get me a lemonade." If I allow it to happen with one of my brothers, or my wife, no one finds it humorous— nor do I believe I intend it to be. That I ever thought there was something to laugh about is beyond embarrassing. For me, "Get me a lemonade" has become a tribute, perhaps; an admission, certainly. It had been unintentional, but I had hurt gentle Leo.

A simple act of kindness, by far more powerful than a thousand voices saying, "Good morning, Leo" and "How are you, Leo?" Nothing more than a sweet lemonade, not too much ice.

LESSONS FROM MY FATHER:
PHIL, JODY, AND DON

It was a mistake, that lunch on a weekend in 1959. I was sixteen when we entered a nondescript, chrome and plastic Howard Johnson's. My father and I were the only customers sitting at the counter, and that made me even more uncomfortable than did the too-small, rotating stools. The waitress handed us oversized, plastic-coated menus and walked away to fill ketchup bottles. The menus were filled with photographs of meals and side orders, and descriptions that had to have been concocted by a junior advertising associate who never had eaten the stuff.

"That hot dog looks pretty good," my father said.

I found the hot dog on my own menu, and it did look good, with diagonal, dark grill marks, nestled in a golden toasted bun, centered on a white plate with a garnish of pickles and lettuce. The accompanying generous glass of cola was another lovely touch.

"Uhhh, are you sure?" I said, certain the hot dog would bear no resemblance to the one on the menu.

I ordered a hamburger. He ordered the dog. He would not be happy with his meal, I would not be happy with his not being happy, and the waitress would not be happy that we had chosen to sit there in the first place.

Our meals arrived. He stared at his plate. "What is this?" he said, looking down at the soft, untoasted hot dog bun, in which had been placed a pink, steamed hot dog on a plate with no decorative garnish.

"A hot dog, sir. The one you ordered."

"That's not the one I ordered. Mine was supposed to be like the photograph," he said.

"Sir, I'm sorry. That's the way we serve them," the waitress said, and retreated down the empty counter to move some things around.

Father controlled his temper. Son was relieved. We sat in silence, nursing private thoughts. Chief among mine, as Son, was, "I don't want you to eat that hot dog. I'm glad you were annoyed about how it looks on the plate."

I didn't want to see what I saw. What sixteen-year-old boy would want to see the father he loves transform into the father he fears, the one whose temper could erupt and eclipse his humor, his patience, his sensitive and caring way of relating to others? My anxiety rose as I recalled instance after instance when I had witnessed his anger, and I knew from experience it could be redirected at me. But, on this day he seemed determined not to embarrass his son or anyone else, including himself.

He ate his hot dog. I ate my hamburger.

It's much more pleasant for me to become immersed in memories of him as our Little League coach and as the scoutmaster of our Boy Scout troop. He found great pleasure in being a teacher and a role model for how to be fair and be a friend.

One of the boys, Phil, from a neighborhood near our

own, had been the catalyst for forming our Little League team. None of the rest of us kids knew Phil very well, and on the day we were to choose the captain, my father made brief, introductory remarks. He told us that when we choose the captain, we should remember who worked the hardest for us to be together as a team. Of course, we ignored the advice of the elder, and no doubt hurt Phil, the one who had worked the hardest.

That was sixty-six years ago, as I write. I have never forgotten that moment, nor have I ever forgotten that my father said nothing to criticize those of us who had ignored his suggestion. He only said something like, "Let's take the field." I imagine him with his arm around Phil's shoulder as they walk toward the diamond. Not long after, I accepted Phil's invitation for a sleepover at his family's beautiful home. We stayed friends for a while, but drifted apart because we attended different schools; I guess we had to work too hard to stay in touch.

As scoutmaster, my father taught us to pitch our green canvas army tents and trench them to divert rainwater, tie an amazing array of knots, sharpen axes without cutting our fingers, build a fire and cook over and under its coals once they acquired a thin layer of gray-white ash. He taught us to slow-cook a hunter stew of beef, carrots, onions, and potatoes. Expecting nothing in return, he helped pay for Boy Scout membership fees, gear, and uniforms for kids in families with even less than we had.

"I'd like you to come with me to talk with Jody and his

dad at their apartment," he said to me one evening after dinner. Jody's family lived in a very small, modest apartment. I don't remember that the mother was there that evening, nor do I remember if there was a mother in the family at all. My father had told me that Jody's dad made very little money, and they'd need some help so his son could become a scout.

I observed how he eased into explaining to the other father that there were available funds to help cover expenses. I also observed the other father's delight when he realized his son would be a scout, and Jody's delight when he realized he'd be one of the kids in the troop, not someone on the outside looking in.

I understood that my father had been suggesting I might befriend this boy who was new to the community. A lot of us scouts did that. I was twelve years old and had the privilege of learning from a master how to help others without diminishing their dignity and pride.

Twenty years later, while in Florida with my father, we had dinner one evening with his best buddy from their time together as soldiers in Europe during WWII. He and my father reminisced about that other type of troop, not one for Boy Scouts, but one that moved east through France and Germany, including during part of the bitter winter of 1944-45.

"You know," Sid said and leaned across the table toward me, as if he were about to say something that must be heard. And it was important, and I did hear it. "It was terrible in the winter over there, but your dad would get in and warm up my sleeping bag and then clear out so I could get in. That's how I could fall asleep. I grew up here in Florida, and never got used to the cold."

During that same Summer of the Hot Dog, I worked
again at my parents' store, as I had the year before, with
Leo. Each year, during the oppressive St. Louis summers,
our main activity was cleaning and storing our customers'
fur garments. When our small, cold storage room couldn't
accommodate any more, we'd use the storage space we
rented in a local department store.

On a blazing day, when asphalt stuck to the soles of
shoes, my father and I walked to the rented space to take
inventory. We'd soon be in the cold, dry air, always welcome
on this kind of day. When we arrived, Don, a young man in
his mid- to late-twenties, greeted us with a huge smile and a
cheerful attitude, as he always did.

I once had heard someone speculate that he might have
a "bit of a mental challenge," but I just thought he was a
kind soul with a gentle demeanor, pleased to serve others in
a gracious way. We had been there several times before, and
he always was happy to see my father, who treated him with
patience and kindness. I took notice of that because there
had been so many times when my father had responded to
other people with anger for perceived slights that could have
been overlooked.

"Can you let us in, Don? Probably for a couple of hours,"
my father said.

He unlocked the heavy door, its protective grillwork
and wires connected to the alarm system that an employee
would activate at the end of a workday.

"You guys know what to do. Just ring the bell inside by

the door when you're ready to leave." He flipped to the ON position the light switches on the wall outside of the vault and closed the door.

Even more than the cold, dry air, it was the earthy aroma from racks of clean garments that was most pleasing to me. Decades later, I still have deep regrets that our family was in that business and that I was one of the participants; but the aroma remains one of my earliest and most comforting memories.

My father and I worked for a couple of hours, taking inventory and making sure the numbers on the tags of hundreds of garments were in the right order. It was approaching five o'clock when we were finishing the last of the twenty-foot-long racks.

"Hey, Dad. Are you as cold as I am?"

"What cannot be cured, must be endured," he said, using the favorite aphorism of Dave Berger.

"Not *that* again. I'm goddamn freezing," I said.

"Well, me too. We're done. I'll ring the bell for Don."

Before we could reach the door, the fluorescent lights above every aisle flickered and went dark. There was as much light in the vault as you could expect to find after making successive right and left turns in a subterranean cavern and arriving at a dead end.

We groped our way down the main aisle that led to the door. Which was locked. From the outside. The layers of weather insulation and the hundreds of garments provided so much soundproofing that the silence was as profound as the darkness.

My father found the button for the bell that Don said

we should ring, so we knew he'd hear it and be back any minute. Though my father had been a radio operator in the combat engineers and was still proficient in Morse code, he didn't signal dit-dit-dit (S) dah-dah-dah (O) dit-dit-dit (S). Instead, he just held his finger on the button for a few seconds, a few times.

Pressing our ears to the door, we could hear a faint sound of the bell. He pressed the button, again. And again. And again. We waited a few short minutes before he rang, again. The creativity of our cursing increased with each episode of bell-ringing. I hoped that my father recognized how much I had learned from him, though not in training sessions approved by the Boy Scouts of America. For this, there was no official merit badge.

"Let's put on some coats," my teacher said.

My father was a smoker. Remembering he had a matchbook in his pocket, he lit one so we were able to find our way to the nearest rack with full-length garments. Each of us chose one, but they were tight around the chest and waist, with sleeves that didn't make it anywhere near our wrists. But, the coats were a blessing; if you kept moving and hugging yourself, the cold and dark were almost tolerable. We talked about piling garments on the floor for a mattress and covering ourselves with layers of other garments if we had to sleep in the vault, something that was becoming more probable as time passed.

He felt his way up and down nearby aisles, and I followed him. Each match provided brief light until the next match would have to be lit. Luck was with us, and high on a wall we found something that looked like an alarm module. He lit a series of matches in an attempt to set off the alarm, but there was no sound at all, other than a word or phrase he used when a match burned his fingertips. This was another lesson. Great material, beyond Tenderfoot, Second Class, even First Class rank. This was pure Eagle Scout.

A few minutes later, we did hear a thudding on the door and a muffled sound that we assumed was a voice. Then, *mirabile dictu*, the lights came on, one by one, flickering at first, and then shining bright as day . . . but not as warm. After what had felt like a long night outside in the freezing cold—but turned out to have been about a half hour—the door opened. We were still in our coats and facing the doorway, eager to get out and get warm and get going. Standing in front of us, on the warm side of the doorway, was none other than Don.

"What are you doing here?" he asked, the way you would ask an acquaintance you meet somewhere you don't expect that person to be, say, Novosibirsk, Siberia, which is the sort of place our time in the frigid air had felt like.

"What are we *doing* here?" my father said, incredulous. I worried that I knew what would happen next. How could I forget the Howard Johnson's hot dog and the waitress who had served it. But, this time it was different. There was not a hint of anger or criticism or anything else that might embarrass the young man, even when he said, in his customary pleasant and friendly tone, "I thought you both had left."

"We always tell you when we leave," my father said in a soft voice, "but, we hadn't left, Don. You must have come up here and locked the door anyway. And you switched off the lights."

"I don't know why, but I thought you had left."

My dad didn't even ask, "Why did you think that?" He just thanked him for rescuing us and said we'd see him again soon.

I was relieved that with Don, my father wasn't angry; he didn't feel helpless, diminished, or humiliated. In fact, by his mood and the way he started to joke about the incident, he seemed to feel that what had happened had been a funny story to be retold many times at the family dinner table: how he and his son were dressed in women's garments, in the middle of the afternoon, locked and freezing in a pitch-dark vault.

We were more than ready to leave and walk back to the store. As we did, we laughed about what had happened. On any other day, what would have been the near-intolerable heat of downtown St. Louis, instead was a warm and welcome caress.

AS ELEMENTARY AS BLACK AND WHITE

St. Louis, *circa* 1950. I love Mrs. Iris Banks, and Mrs. Iris Banks loves me. She is, in a way, part of our family. While my parents are at work, she helps raise my brothers and me in our all-white neighborhood.

In her forties, her face has a delicate beauty; her brown skin is luminous. She is thin, even slight, and wears simple cotton dresses with pads in the shoulders. Her black hair is parted in the middle and gathered in a loose bun. I'm a little boy, six or seven years old, on that summer day when my mother is home and Iris Banks brings her niece to our apartment. We're the same six or seven years old, and our two families have decided we should play together. She wears a pretty white dress, and her black hair is pulled back in braids. Her Auntie Iris and my mother tell us to walk to the drugstore, sit at the counter, and have something cold to drink.

This is *circa* 1950 St. Louis, when people the skin color of my playmate and her Auntie Iris are permitted to sit only in top balconies of those "white" movie theaters that admit them. To get to the drugstore, Iris Banks's niece and I must walk down the alley behind our apartment building. The alley is a favorite hangout for neighborhood kids, none of whom are around that day. There are ash pits for bonfires, dark garages for hideouts during Cops and Robbers, and tons of rocks, which have become golf balls to smack with a bent, left-handed club we've found near a trash can. The alleys are linear playgrounds, pathways to safe places where, on ordinary days, no harm is done to anyone.

Clutching the coins my mother handed me, I lead the way down our alley that passes by the loading dock of the grocery store, where slatted wooden crates emit the unmistakable odor of discarded produce sitting in the summer heat. We hurry through the store's parking lot, turn left at the sidewalk, and arrive at the drugstore. Even there, no other kids are around. Frightened that the drugstore adults will be angry if my playmate and I enter together, I think I'm protecting her—and myself—when I tell her to wait outside. And she does, alone on a wide sidewalk in a strange neighborhood, just a little girl in a pretty white dress and her black hair pulled back in braids. Inside, I ask for two colas, and a woman places them on the tan marble counter where I have spread out my nickels and dimes. I drop a straw into each paper cone. Careful not to squeeze, I lift them from their hourglass-shaped, metal holders. Using my hip and shoulder to open the heavy glass swinging door, I carry the drinks outside, and we sip them while retracing our steps past the decaying produce, dark garages, and ash pits, until we're safe at home.

Almost seventy years have disappeared since that ill-conceived adventure. Had my mother and Auntie Iris not considered their two little innocents might have been ordered to leave the drugstore? And then what? I live in another city now, with its own alleys. I need only to walk by one to wonder if Iris Banks's niece remembers me as the boy who had tried to protect her—and himself—or the boy who had done nothing but abandon her on the sidewalk. And why don't I even remember her name? Does she even remember me, at all?

More than often, I reimagine that summer day so very long ago.

Iris Banks's niece skips as we rush down the alley to Citron's drugstore. The woman who makes our drinks places the paper cones, secure in their metal hourglass holders, on the tan marble counter where I have spread out our nickels and dimes. My playmate and I giggle as we twist left and right on the revolving stools and enjoy our drinks. When just the right amount of cola remains in the paper cones, our straws make that awesome sound kids love and grown-ups can't stand. We laugh at this and know we've become friends.

A little boy in shorts, and a little girl in a pretty white dress and her black hair pulled back in braids, take their sweet time walking up the alley, holding hands all the way home.

And then there was Devon Paris. The year was 1956, and people like Devon and Iris's niece were still referred to in St. Louis, and elsewhere, as "colored people." To its credit, the Supreme Court had ruled two years earlier that our school, among all the others, would be integrated. Thus, Devon became a Boy Scout in our grade school troop. My father was still scoutmaster and would continue to be, even after his three boys were too old for scouting, or no longer interested.

This was my thirteenth summer and my second year with our troop at scout camp. The camp was located in the hills of southeastern Missouri near a town with a population of around five hundred. At the time, the town was nothing at all like the comparatively larger, more cosmopolitan place it has become.

As I remember it from my scouting days, and my memory is incomplete, the few streets were lined with small clapboard or brick houses, a small number of stores, a coffee shop and restaurant, and a blacksmith. The entire area had been the site of numerous Civil War skirmishes; in this border state of Missouri, it would not have been unusual for friends and family to be on both sides of a fight.

In 1956, the town people were used to scouts walking their streets, hiking on the nearby two-lane, blacktop highway, and adding to the local economy. Among many of us from the "big city," the area had a reputation as racist and intolerant, though we had no firsthand experiences to justify that reputation.

As part of the program for the week at scout camp, our troop observed a tradition of taking a five-mile hike, with packs on our backs, to a waterfall and swimming hole where we would camp overnight. To get there, we would have to pass through the town, which we did in formation, marching two abreast.

My father, who had returned eleven years earlier from World War II, marched on our right flank. As we approached the town, he slowed his pace to walk by my side. He suggested to a few of us older scouts marching close together—all of us the ripe old age of thirteen—that we should be ready to protect Devon if we were attacked. After all, the Boy Scout motto means what it says: "Be Prepared."

To live up to the motto, we did what all good scouts would have done: We removed our short-handle, standard-issue Boy Scout axes from the sheaths on our belts and held the weapons as low as possible in a determined, but laughable attempt at conceal-carry. Most of us were dressed in standard-issue Boy Scout shorts, so the axes were more than a little conspicuous against our bare legs.

We kept our heads facing forward, while our eyes scanned the possible field of battle. Devon Paris and the rest of our troop marched through the town like General Sherman through Georgia. I don't recall that we saw anyone at all; it seemed that every fearful man, woman, and child had retreated indoors, closed the curtains, and stole furtive peeks at the invading Children's Army. This was one Civil War skirmish the North won, hands down.

Ten years later, in 1966, I returned to visit that town. Two friends had joined me on a weekend camping trip at the site they had heard me talk about in glowing terms, many times. But when we were driving the two-lane blacktop and getting closer to the town, I began to feel an uneasiness that I fought to dispel. I was afraid. This felt like enemy territory.

Before heading to the campsite, we stopped in the town so I could find the blacksmith who had lived there since forever. When we arrived, he was standing outside. He was a gray-haired man in overalls who looked to be in his late fifties, at least. He stood bent forward slightly from the waist as if he had some sort of problem with his back. We said hello, and I asked if he still had a grinding wheel to sharpen my Boy Scout axe, the same one I had when I was a scout.

"Sure do," he said.

My friends waited outside as he led me through his yard and into his shop, more like a small, weathered barn. The dust in the air sparkled in the sunbeams that penetrated the few cloudy windows. I had to walk stooped over like he did in order to pass under several low, thick beams. We stopped in front of the old grinding wheel, and he began to work on my axe with an ease that had come from years of holding blades at just the right angle while turning the arm of the wheel at just the right speed. Brilliant yellow and white sparks cascaded from the wheel and blade and were extinguished on the dirt floor.

Concentrating on the work in front of him, and raising his voice above the noise of the wheel on steel, the blacksmith said, "Can I ask you something?"

"Sure you can."

"Is that war in Korea over? Who won?"

"Well, we did, sort of." I didn't tell him the fighting had ended thirteen years earlier.

When the blacksmith had given the blade a shiny, new edge, he let the wheel slow to a stop. He raised the blade to eye level and regarded his work; he was pleased. I don't know how much I paid him, but I hope it was more than enough.

It was mid-afternoon when my friends and I left the town and drove down another two-lane blacktop road toward the waterfall, a mile or two away. My earlier uneasiness increased to a level I believed was completely unreasonable, but that didn't stop me from fantasizing that we could wind up being prey for predatory locals.

A few places along the road looked familiar, but it was hard to discern where the path to the waterfall and campsite met the two-lane county highway. After several failed attempts, we found the path, and I parked on the shoulder as far as possible from the road.

It took two trips for us to carry our gear to the campsite, where the stream runs through the woods and red granite hills, and tumbles over a waterfall about twenty feet high. At the bottom of the falls, a deep pool about fifteen feet wide and five feet deep had been formed by the force of the water and the damming effect of the granite boulders. Scouts who camped at this site would cool off in that pool, with its steady supply of fresh, clean water from the stream that continued its journey to a maze of other waterways that led to the Mississippi, where Tom and Huck and Jim had floated years before.

We had been setting up camp under the mid-afternoon, southern Missouri sun, when one of my friends, Mickey, said, "Let's just stop and go for a swim."

"Good idea," I said. "Then, we can lie on the hot granite."

Mickey and I stripped to our underwear. So did our friend, Susan. I led the way down the smooth, red boulders that lined both sides of the falls.

"What the . . . Holy crap. C'mere and look at this."

Mickey and Susan made their way to where I stood on a granite boulder. The swimming hole was occupied by locals, but not the ones I had unreasonably feared. The sight of a large mass of what I remember as greenish-brown water snakes writhing around, over and under each other, was appalling. In the intense heat, I shivered.

"Uhhh . . . guess what?" Susan said. "We're not going swimming today."

In spite of our disappointment, we decided not to leave. We rested, talked, and waded in the stream as it flowed over the flat ledge just before tumbling over the falls. When it was time to prepare a late dinner, Mickey, a chef in training, cooked our vegetables and meat over the wood fire. I prepared some quick-bake bread from a mix by wrapping the dough in tinfoil and burying it in the coals. By the time dinner was ready, the concoction was a thick, inedible paste, which, of course, Chef Mickey had warned me would be the inevitable outcome.

When darkness fell, we lay on our bedrolls under a cloudless sky as the full moon rose. Its cold, white light washed out almost all of the stars and lent everything around us a ghostly cast. Since my first sight of the swarm of snakes, the campsite, the waterfall and swimming hole, and the little Missouri town had lost their allure. The local residents had done nothing I was aware of to warrant my fear; nevertheless, I attached it to them, and it was palpable and unshakable.

Though *Deliverance* wouldn't be published for four more years, and the movie wouldn't be released for two more years after that, both versions of the story would remind me of what I had feared in and around that small Missouri town. I was thirteen years old again, marching with my Boy Scout hatchet against my bare leg, trying to be prepared, but knowing we couldn't be.

Well before dawn, the moon had dropped low in the sky, and we were awakened by snarls and growls and the sound of a trash can tipping over. It was dark enough that we couldn't determine what kind of animals had visited us, but we knew there had been more than one. In the light of morning, we discovered that they had eaten or carried away almost every scrap of food, paper, and other trash. Nothing was left but a few empty tin cans and bottles—and my ersatz bread. The visitors had opened the foil wrap a few inches, but hadn't been desperate enough to sample what was inside.

We broke camp and drove home.

I've never returned to that campsite, where the stream runs through the woods and red granite hills, and tumbles over a waterfall about twenty feet high.

VIETNAM AT 20,000 FEET

Summer 1987. "We have a problem, sir, and we need you to change your seat. I'm very sorry for the inconvenience, but you'll have to move to the window seat."

I'd boarded the plane early, stowed my suitcase, and could not have been more content, considering I had been upgraded to first class and assigned the seat I had requested—aisle, bulkhead, with maximum legroom. I knew I'd be comfortable and wouldn't have to deal with the inconvenience of climbing over anyone's legs in order to use the restroom. After all, I was one of those forty-four-year-old guys in an expensive suit, on my way to one of those "really important trips" to New York.

"Why do I have to move? There are other seats open in first class."

"We specifically need yours."

"I did everything I could to reserve this seat, and now you're saying you need it for one of your special customers?"

"Yes, that's correct, sir."

As I began to say something more, I noticed what was happening behind her, by the entry door. A man my age was in the aisle. He was several feet tall, and his head reached not far above the armrests of the passenger seats on either side of him. From his head down, his body ended at the few inches that remained of what had been his legs. He propelled himself by pressing his fists against the floor, boosting his torso about six inches, swinging forward as far as his arms and momentum would permit, landing on the floor, and then repeating the series of well-practiced moves, all the while smiling at anyone he saw watching him, myself included. Ashamed of my self-absorbed interaction with the flight attendant, I lifted the armrest and scooted over to the window seat.

The passenger arrived at his and my row and said, "Thanks, man. I'm really sorry you had to move."

"It's no problem at all." I was uneasy about how he intended to get from the floor to the seat. "Would you like me to help you?"

"Nope. I'm fine. Watch."

He propelled himself the remaining, short distance to his aisle seat and used the same technique to pivot so his back was against the front of the seat cushion. He lifted his arms behind him and placed the heels of his hands on either side of the cushion. His shirtsleeves were rolled to the elbows, revealing his heavily muscled forearms and the thick calluses on his knuckles and other parts of his hands. With a powerful push, he boosted himself onto the seat and fastened his belt for takeoff.

"I have a lot of practice," he said, flashing that great smile.

"I guess you do. You're really good at it."

After takeoff, we began a conversation. He told me he was a Vietnam combat veteran, and I asked him if he'd mind telling me how he'd been wounded.

"It wasn't complicated. I was in one of the trucks of a long convoy, and we hit a land mine. The blast blew me out of the truck, and the next thing I knew, I was in the hospital. You can see what happened."

"I do see." And what I saw was heartbreaking.

I'm in my first year of college. It's 1960, before Vietnam will become a name connected to so much pain and sorrow, fear and anger. The college has an ROTC program that all first- and second-year students must participate in. Every week, I amass demerits for not completing classwork assignments, not spit-shining my black shoes, not polishing my brass buttons, not cleaning my M-1 rifle well enough. And more. Once a week, we have drill practice. On one of those days, Colonel Donner looks in my direction and asks for a volunteer from the platoon I'm in to lead the men through drill. He's flanked by his junior officer and by advanced cadets, all of whom are surprised when I volunteer. They smirk, knowing I'll be humiliated. Their expressions fade as our platoon marches perfectly—right flank, left flank, column right and column left, oblique right and left, halt, left face, right face, about face, dress right dress, present arms, right shoulder arms, left face, forward march— all around the large field and back to where we began. I report to the colonel and salute as required. He asks how I learned all of this. I tell him my father was in Patton's Third Army not long before, and then was our scoutmaster and taught us how to drill and enjoy it. More like a team sport than a preparation for war. A few days later, the colonel asks me to report to his office. He asks why I object to being trained as a soldier when, after all, "Your people were warriors. Maccabees, right?" What

I want to ask, but don't, is how does he know I'm Jewish, and why does he think it's particularly relevant? I'm pleased that at least he refers to Maccabees and not to the Holocaust and gas chambers and the trope that Jews did nothing but march obediently to their deaths. His words matter, though. I enjoyed leading the platoon in the drill. I even want to learn much of what the program has to teach. Maybe be a warrior. Like my father had been. But I have a different fight to fight. Leaving my father's shadow, as it were. His anger. His often abusive behavior. All part of what must have been for me the confusing picture of what a soldier is.

"I'm very sorry that happened to you," was all I thought my Vietnam veteran fellow passenger would appreciate, if anything at all.

In an intimate act that surprised me, he gestured towards his crotch. "Yeah, I'm kind of messed up down there. I mean, I can do things to take care of myself, but the rest of it . . . you know what I mean." He gave another of his smiles that made me love this guy, not pity him. He and I alternated between talking and retreating into our own thoughts during the remainder of the flight from St. Louis to New York.

1966, and my undergraduate college fails to send the draft board some necessary documents, so the draft board cancels my student deferment, and I receive the dreaded "Greetings" letter informing me of the day, time, and place for the physical exam for my induction into the army. I report to the draft board building (where war protestors demonstrate on a somewhat regular basis and, once in a while, have bags of urine dropped on their heads, but not on mine—I demonstrated elsewhere). Next to the large room where we are to gather after we "prepare for the exam," another draftee and I stand near each other, strip to our underwear, and put our clothes in metal lockers. It's impossible not to notice his artificial leg below the knee. I ask him why he's here, and he says he tried to explain it to the draft board, but they told him to go to the physical and tell the story to the doctors. I pass the exam and am classified I-A (prime material). Days before I'm to report for induction and to take the oath, the document confusion is resolved and my deferment and 2-S classification are reinstated. That's the end of my time in the military.

I wondered if my fellow passenger might be curious if I had served during the war, because we were about the same age. I considered asking if he had been drafted or had enlisted, but I wanted to avoid what could turn out to be an "America, right or wrong" debate about patriotism. Had that conversation taken place, I would have told him that on the day of my induction I would be in Canada or on my way to jail for refusing, conscientiously, to take the oath and the requisite step forward.

I'm in my mid-thirties, sitting in an airplane next to a middle-aged woman in the window seat. As night falls, we begin a conversation somewhere over Kansas. Her view is better than mine, but both of us are able to see at least a dozen miniature Fourth of July firework displays thousands of feet below us, spread over a wide swath of rural Kansas. She turns away from the window and begins a story. She's wistful, even melancholy, as she tells me she was born and raised in a small Kansas town, like the ones so far below us. On the Fourth of July, everyone turned out for the parade, the picnic, and the fireworks.

"Do you know why I loved the holiday so much? I was born on the Fourth of July." She turns again to the window, and a long, few seconds later, she says, "Yes, I was."

"Well, happy birthday to you. I've never met anyone born on the Fourth of July," I say. "Was that a lot of fun for you?"

"Oh, yes. It really was." She laughs, still looking out the window. Then she turns to me. "I think I was eight years old before I knew or, I guess, really believed, that the parade and fireworks weren't for my birthday."

I glanced at my war veteran, fellow passenger who, eyes closed, was dozing or just thinking, as I had been. I don't remember what I was thinking about, but it's easy to imagine it was that little girl in Kansas on the Fourth of July, holding a cone of melting, vanilla ice cream, America's favorite flavor, no longer feeling part of the parade, no longer enjoying the Sousa march while she looked at the American flags and the men in uniform. That's what many of us felt during the Vietnam War when we experienced what we believed was a distorted patriotism. America—Love it or Leave it. A war for what? In the end, was anything about it worth what happened to the man sitting next to me on the plane?

Our flight landed, and we remained seated while others began to disembark.

"I enjoyed sitting with you," I said.

"Yeah. I enjoyed it, too. Take it easy, man."

We shook hands, our grips steady and tight. His calluses felt good, not as rough as I'd expected. Without any of the inconvenience I had so wanted to avoid, I walked in front of him and removed my bag from the overhead compartment. We exchanged a smile before I moved down the aisle, wondering how he'd get off the plane.

At the end of the walkway into the terminal, an airline employee stood next to a wheelchair. Would he roll it to the airplane door or to the veteran's seat? Would the soldier propel himself to the terminal and hoist himself onto the chair waiting there for him? I wanted to return and tell him again how sorry I was that he had suffered such grievous wounds, to tell him everything I had been thinking about on the airplane. But that seemed the wrong thing to do.

I'd been so disturbed that another person needed to take my treasured aisle seat, the same person who also had taken what might have been my seat in a truck that would be blown up by a land mine. Walking through the terminal, I wondered why the veteran's strong, callused hands had been so comforting, so reassuring. I told myself it was because they communicated his strength and resilience. Anyway, that's what I wanted it to be. Otherwise, it would have been even harder to deal with a stark reality:

I did not go to Vietnam, he did; I walked off the airplane, he did not.

EXODUS REDUX

"It was just like Isaac," I said.

"Yes. We were sacrificed."

"Yes. Sacrificial lambs."

"Exactly."

This is how my older brother and I began a conversation about the school that he and I attended, along with our younger brother.

Genesis. In the beginning of the 1947-48 school year, I attended a Jewish parochial school with a name that took forever to say: The Rabbi H. F. Epstein Hebrew Academy. Often "shortened" by omitting "Rabbi," the Academy was the first Jewish day school in Missouri, founded in 1943, the year of my birth. My two brothers—one three years older, the other four years younger—also attended the Academy. The older brother would complete grade school there, I would attend from kindergarten through the fifth grade, and the younger brother would attend for only a part of the kindergarten school year.

Each morning, we recited prayers and studied the *Torah*, other aspects of Judaism, and the Hebrew language.

Each afternoon, we shifted to the standard Missouri school curriculum. My grades were good; there were teachers I liked; I had friends. I like to say their names: Doreen, Adele, Miriam, Benjie, Jeff, Harold, Ronnie, Joshua, and Karen.

A few names stand out to me. Ronnie was the friend I would hang out with on many weekends. From early in grade school, Joshua's serious demeanor and penchant to give *Torah* lessons were befitting of what lay in store for him. He already was the son of the chief orthodox rabbi in St. Louis. Karen was the girl who always had my full attention, even when I wasn't with her. She had big brown eyes, and shiny, dark brown hair she wore in bangs. I mean, I really loved Karen. On the school bus, I pulled her hair.

On balance, though, the Rabbi H. F. Epstein Hebrew Academy was a childhood experience that came with a cost too high for me to bear. What had begun as a vague feeling of resentment, by the third grade would begin to acquire significant clarity; each painful day I boarded a school bus headed for the Hebrew Academy was another day that marked me as "different," an "outsider." And a traumatic encounter with a school authority would intensify those feelings.

My family had moved to one of the units in a six-family apartment building that my maternal grandparents helped purchase. The building was across the street from a wonderful public school and its playground, one the neighborhood kids loved and I envied. They walked to school—some no further than across the street—while I had to walk to the corner and wait for the school bus to take me somewhere I did not want to be taken.

Even though I had made friends with some of the kids, even though groups of us would hang out together, I never experienced the pleasure and the security that would have come from being their classmate, from truly being one of the gang. In my child's mind, the Rabbi H. F. Epstein Hebrew Academy itself kept me an outsider in my own neighborhood.

My parents' decision to send my brothers and me to that school carried an important historical context. My maternal grandparents had emigrated from Poland to America early in the twentieth century and had left behind many of their extended family members, a few of whom survived beyond the end of World War II. My father had been an American soldier in France and Germany when what was happening in the concentration camps became widely known. Following the Holocaust, Jews throughout the world, including my grandparents and parents, understood that sacrifices, financial and other, would be needed to ensure the future of the Jewish people.

In spite of all of this, I don't believe my parents would have decided on their own that enrolling their children in a Jewish parochial school was essential to achieving that goal; there must have been considerable pressure from my mother's parents. Though my parents were, I believe, ambivalent about the school, nothing deterred four elders from continuing to send three boys as sacrifices on the altar of the Rabbi H. F. Epstein Hebrew Academy.

And so it was written. And so it came to pass. I would be forlorn whenever I would watch the kids on their paved playground with painted lines for volleyball, kickball, basketball, football, softball, and hopscotch. I wanted to be one of those kids. Some of them were Jewish, but they didn't have to wear a *yarmulke* and *tzitzis* (with its four corners under the shirt and knotted strings hanging outside).

On many weekends and evenings, when the gates in the tall chain-link fence that surrounded the playground were locked, kids would climb over and continue their games. I sometimes joined them, but those brief moments of camaraderie weren't enough to counter the painful reality of my isolation and loneliness. I often felt like a waif who wanders the streets of Old London at Christmas, his sooty face pressed against the outside of the candy store window. I'm sure that this feeling was intensified knowing, as I did, that my younger brother had left the Hebrew Academy after a very short stay, and had been enrolled in the school I longed to attend. My parents must have begun to resolve their ambivalence about the importance of a parochial school education, but it would take at least another year for me to benefit from this change.

The Rabbi H. F. Epstein Hebrew Academy didn't waste its limited budget on proper playgrounds. At its first location, there was a dirt play area. My classmates and I were little kids, at most in the third grade, and we had no athletic equipment other than some soccer-size rubber balls and marble collections some of the boys brought from home in drawstring bags. We would scratch a circle in the dirt and kneel around it, as serious as men at an alley crap game. The only difference was we played with glass "peewees" and "boulders."

The best thing the play area did have to offer was a treasure trove of rocks. We improvised. One otherwise normal day, about a dozen boys and a few girls lined up on two sides. I don't remember who it was that threw first, but when my rock hit my friend Harold high in the center of his forehead, blood flowed down his face and decorated his white shirt. We all froze. Everyone stared at Harold and his bloody face and shirt, and at me as I stared at Harold, while Harold just stared. Trapped on a small, fenced-in playground far from our homes, I have no idea where we thought we might hide

After murdering his brother Abel, Cain must have experienced a similar sense of panic. His dissembling before an omniscient God served only to make a bad situation worse. Unlike Abel, Harold lived. That's why he, though bleeding, could run into the school building.

I expected to hear, as did Cain, a thunderous voice emanating from nowhere and everywhere: "Who was it that endeavored to slay Master Harold?" As I already predicted—"prophesied" would be more in keeping with the school's orientation—I was the only child blamed. Someone had ratted on me, or I had been frightened enough to confess my sin. Regardless, I was the child who had dispatched the rock on its true path, during an event that bore no resemblance whatsoever to the slaying of Goliath.

Someone old, like one of the Sanhedrin in the ancient Jerusalem temple, told me to report to the High Priest, cleverly disguised as the school superintendent. Huge and intimidating, Rabbi Kuglowski led me to the basement.

Isaac must have felt something similar to my own trepidation when Abraham suggested they go for a little stroll up the mountain to offer a sacrifice. There was that moment when the son wondered aloud why the father had remembered the wood, fire, and knife, but had forgotten the lamb—at least not the four-legged variety. As they ascended, we can hope that Isaac had trust in Abraham and was assured by his father's words of faith, "God will provide himself a lamb . . ." But as the superintendent and I descended, following his less assuring "Come downstairs with me," I had no such trust. Certain there was no lamb in our basement or anywhere else in the building, I didn't have to wonder aloud whether I was in big trouble.

Rabbi Kuglowski led me to an unoccupied room, where we faced each other on chairs he moved away from a table. Without taking time to introduce the concept of repentance—a concept that had been given such importance by no less than the Jewish sage Maimonides in the middle of the twelfth century—the Patriarch Kuglowski raised his hand and slapped me across my face.

A little boy, unprotected, feeling abandoned, frightened, like a bleating lamb—feelings that were too familiar to me.

I don't remember if I said anything to my parents about what had happened between the rabbi and me, but it's hard for me to imagine I said nothing. I also don't know if the rabbi told them. In either case, what happened in that room never has left me. I'm sure that *home* and *school* merged, each reinforcing the other, both confirming to me, even at my young age, that something was very wrong and I was helpless to change it. Though I remained in the Academy for several more years without another incident like the one in the basement, my need to escape never diminished.

Exodus to a land of milk and honey. In 1953, at the end of my fifth grade year, and not a moment too soon, my parents decided we would move to a different neighborhood and their children would leave the Rabbi H. F. Epstein Hebrew Academy. The timing was right. My older brother would begin high school; my younger brother would have a chance to spend his grade school years not having to climb over a playground fence; I would be relieved of a sadness that had become extreme, and would be able to end my isolation from neighborhood kids.

I now wonder about those moments when I learned we were moving. Did I fantasize that I would lead the entire student body in a reenactment of the Exodus from Egypt? Would we have encountered that troublesome Red Sea? Would there have been an army of angry parents and rabbis chasing us on chariots? And, if so, who or what would have saved us?

There is a small problem with this then-or-now fantasy. I don't recall my classmates demonstrating anything similar to the suffering of his people in bondage that Moses had witnessed, as it is said. Even if my classmates had felt oppressed, they would have been as afraid as I would have been to just get up and walk out the door. It's possible that something surprising would have happened had I risen from my school desk and said to my people, "Let's flee this place of bondage and suffering. There's a better place not far from here, but we'll have to walk. Who's with me? How about you, Karen?" Joshua could have helped by being my right-hand man, like Aaron was to Moses, but he most likely never would have left, not even if he could play the part of Moses, a part for which he already was more spiritually qualified than I was. It stands to reason that he would become an orthodox rabbi as his father was before him.

Alas, my personal exodus was far more mundane, but still exciting. Our family moved only a couple of miles, but it was to a neighborhood within the same district as the public school I had admired. Our apartment now was only three short blocks from my new school, and soon I would walk to a playground that was even better than the one I had envied, the one that had been so emblematic of much that had been missing in my life. This playground had the same markings of yellow, white, and blue stripes, rectangles, circles, and semicircles, but its fence was only waist-high, and its several gates were never locked. And it was a playground with no rocks.

Karen was still very much in my thoughts as the school year began, so I was surprised by my immediate attraction to a new classmate who differed from her in personality, looks, and style. This girl had long, light brown hair with a little wave that fell over one side of her forehead, and whenever she wore her camel-colored skirt and light beige knee stockings, my attempts at concentration were futile. Because I owned a small pocketknife, it seemed like a good idea to carve her name and mine, with a heart in between, deep into a window frame overlooking the playground.

When I was called to the principal's office, I was surprised by how he had been able to identify the love-struck culprit.

"How did you know I did it?"

"There were two clues," Mr. Henderson said. "First, you carved your own name. Second—and this is more than a clue, I suppose—everyone saw you do it."

In spite of his gentle way of speaking to me, I was sure he was angry. But he wasn't, and he didn't slap me. He said, in the future I should respect other people's property. He said, "You should have known that already," and smiled at me. With that smile, I had all the confirmation I ever would need that I was not in exile, and this school was not the lonely diaspora. No, not at all. Indeed, it was a miracle.

A time to gain and a time to lose. In 2019, at age seventy-six, my view from the Promised Land encompasses not only what I had gained by my solo exodus, but also what I had lost. During the year after I left the R.H.F.E.H.A., I met with Ronnie a few times, and then we drifted apart. I never saw Karen again, or any other of the classmates I had been with since kindergarten. I very often have asked myself why I lost all contact with my classmates, but all I know is that I just moved on, figuratively and literally.

But several months ago, while looking for a misplaced paper, I found a photograph taken in our apartment during my birthday party at age eight or nine. Seven of my classmates are there. Of course, Karen is one of them. We are sitting on a couch and on the floor, and smiling at the camera. Whenever I look at that photograph, I'm reminded of something I have known for the past sixty-six years: I walked away from these earliest of friends, but I never left. I carry them with me now, as I always have. I miss them, even love them.

Nevertheless, it remains as true today as it was then: I knew I had to follow a different path than the one we had been taught was ideal. I was a young boy who yearned for a different sort of Promised Land, and found one—complete with very low, chain-link fences and gates that were never locked, surrounding a clean, smooth, asphalt playground marked with those beautiful, carefully painted, yellow, white, and blue boundary lines, rectangles, circles, and semicircles.

MORE THAN A CUP OF COFFEE

In 1963, what I knew about Israel had been learned by listening to conversations at my grandparents' dinner table. Otherwise, my knowledge and interest were limited to placing coins in a little blue collection box like those found in many Jewish homes for the purpose of buying land in Palestine and supporting subsequent programs in what would become Israel. I also had received certificates on some of my birthdays indicating a tree had been planted in my name or honor or both.

Late in the spring of my third year of college, a flyer posted on a bulletin board advertised a lecture, scheduled for that evening, by a representative from the Israeli consulate in Los Angeles. *What else do I have to do tonight?* I asked myself. *Not much*, I answered.

Because I had been longing to do something, to go somewhere, anywhere, to break the monotonous routine of attending classes, I must have been susceptible to the lecturer's description of Israel, officially recognized only fifteen years earlier. The lecture was propaganda, but it worked on me. He made it seem romantic, dangerous, exciting, and filled with meaning. Just what a languishing, twenty-year-old college student might want to hear, and might want to experience.

I was captivated by the tales of building a country, the pioneering spirit, the constant threat of war with neighboring countries, and the triumph of the underdog after centuries of persecution. I'm certain that this last issue was the one that sealed the deal. Since childhood, I'd been not only aware of anti-Semitism, but had experienced it many times; it had been painful, infuriating, and had begun to feel inexorable.

When the lecture ended, I walked by myself in the clear and warm Colorado night. At a particular tall white pine, where the view to the west was unobstructed, I stopped to appreciate the beauty of Pike's Peak, visible against an early night, cobalt blue sky. At that moment, my decision was made. I figured that the sky and the mountain would be there when I returned.

Within a few weeks, I had arranged with the college administration to leave for at least a year and live in Israel. And that's what I did.

More than a half century later, whenever I think about that year, I'm flooded with memories of the beautiful and the not-so-beautiful scenery, the smells, the sounds, the feel of the dirt and rocks under my sandals, the dust that coated my feet when I walked on trails. I remember the young man I was, and still expect to see, no matter how many times I look at my reflection and am surprised.

In "Dreams of Distant Treks," Eric Shipton captured what I felt then, and feel now:

There is no better way of becoming intimately acquainted with country than by walking over it . . . The springs of enchantment lie within ourselves: they arise from our sense of wonder, that most precious of gifts, the birthright of every child . . . (In Ron Strickland's anthology *Shank's Mare: A Compendium of Remarkable Walks*)

When I arrived in Israel, I purchased a guidebook in a small bookstore that I found while exploring an old neighborhood of Tel Aviv. That guidebook, which I still have, led me through parts of that Mediterranean coastal city and neighboring Jaffa; north along the coast through Caesarea, Acre, Haifa and Mt. Carmel, and Rosh Hanikra where Israel and Lebanon meet overlooking the sea; through Nazareth, Safed, and other parts of the Galilee and the Jezreel Valley; north to Metulah and the border with Lebanon; up to Jerusalem and the surrounding hills and nearby villages; to Bethlehem, and into the Negev desert and Masada, Sodom, and Beer Sheva.

The Jordan Valley, just south of Tiberias and the Sea of Galilee, *Yam Kinneret*, is where I had chosen to live and work on a kibbutz. My first night there, I was awakened many times by the loud reports of a carbide cannon timed to frighten away the occasional wild boar and the more frequent jackals that visited our commercial fish ponds. For the next few nights, the howling and cackling of the jackals were eerie to someone like me who hadn't heard them before, especially not in the late night and early morning darkness. Before long, I'd learn more about those jackals.

After working in the banana fields and citrus orchards for a few months, I had the chance to work in the fish ponds. Raising and harvesting tilapia, also known as "St. Peter's fish," was fascinating, and I was allowed to make this my primary work for much of the remainder of my time in the kibbutz. On many mornings, the three of us on the team would find several dead fish lying on the bank of a pond, each fish killed by two puncture wounds from jackal fangs.

That sight was disturbing to me, not so much because the fish were dead—I'd seen plenty of dead fish in my two decades of life—but that they hadn't been killed for food. Seeing them lying there was a reminder that I was somewhere that was more than new and fascinating to me. It was dangerous. We lived in a time and place of repeated hostilities, sometimes with fatalities, almost always with little or no warning.

One of the more pleasant aspects of working with this small team was that the ponds were close to the Yarmuk, the narrow river that formed the border between Syria and Jordan, and at our kibbutz, the border between us and Jordan. Near our fields, the Yarmuk was only a few yards wide in places, and at most about twenty feet. There was a beautiful, deep swimming hole lined with tall grasses and tropical shrubs and other plants, some with dark pink blossoms. I swam there with a girl from another kibbutz. We hadn't planned on swimming, so we had no suits. At more routine times of any given workday, I would cool myself in the clear water or would just stand on the bank and soak in the beauty. I never stopped wanting to swim and wade across the Yarmuk into Jordan, and walk to one of the small villages on the distant hills.

I often thought about the trip I took a few weeks after I'd arrived in Israel, when someone I'd become friends with took me to her hometown of Metulah, the northernmost point of Israel. Her father had been an early pioneer, was fluent in Arabic, and had befriended many of the original occupants of the land, some of whom were now living in Lebanon, across the border. He led us on a walk through the fields near his modest home and identified the border by reference to landmarks that I had difficulty discerning, even as he pointed to them. To me, the rocks were the same, the trees were the same, and the terrain was same, as far as I could see in all directions. What border?

Later that year, in a field near the swimming hole, I was helping remove rocks the size of golf balls up to cantaloupes, in preparation for tilling and planting. During a break from this important but boring work, I stood by myself and tried to absorb the magnificent scenery that always exhilarated me.

The sparkling-clear, early winter day was warm with low humidity. The panorama began as I turned to face southeast toward the brown and red hills of Jordan with their white and tan stucco dwellings of small villages and the larger town of Irbid. It continued as I turned northeast toward the Golan Heights and the narrow valley between Jordan and Syria through which the Yarmuk River flowed on its journey to my swimming hole and on to its confluence

with the Jordan River. The final turn was to the north, so
I could gaze beyond the green banana fields and orchards
of the Jordan Valley, beyond the Sea of Galilee, beyond
the Hula Valley, beyond Metulah, all the way to Mount
Hermon, its snow-capped summit floating on a low bed of
clouds. Everything was in such relief, it seemed as though I
could reach out my hand and touch what I saw but could
not visit. How odd, how wasteful this hatred and war, these
borders I could not cross.

Two or three months later that winter, four of us were
working for several days close to the Jordanian border, this
time a large wheat field in the Galilee, which we drove to
each morning from our kibbutz in the Jordan Valley. Close
to the field was a small cluster of old, adobe-type homes
where Palestinians still lived. The site of those homes, in
an area that once was populated by a large number of
Palestinians, was, for me, another disturbing reminder of
how close in time we were to what Israelis call the War of
Independence and Palestinians call the *Nakba*, Catastrophe.

That heavy reminder, along with the cold, overcast, and
damp weather, made it even harder to tolerate what was the
most mind-numbing work I ever had done. Four abreast, we
walked, step by step by step by step, back and forth and forth
and back, dunam after dunam, stopping every few feet to dip
a little aluminum spoon into a large tin can each of us carried
filled with kernels of wheat coated in rose-colored poison. At
each stop, we had to drop a few of the poisoned kernels into
tiny holes that were the entrances of field mouse tunnels.

For part of the first day, the process seemed cruel. But I developed a different attitude after hours of walking, staring at the ground, looking for the tiny holes, and stooping and rising every few feet until my back and legs, but mostly what was left of my brain, ached so much that what began as a feeling of compassion and guilt quickly became *If the little menaces insist on eating all the ripening wheat, well . . .* Every few hours, I finished the sentiment with a different phrase.

An elderly Palestinian man lived in one of the houses near the field where we worked; I saw him a few times standing outside of his house and looking in our direction. This might be my imagination, but one day I gave a small wave, which he returned. On our last day, he walked close to where we were working and invited us for coffee. We entered his stone and adobe house, and he led us to a small, dimly lit room with one window and a clean concrete floor. We kept our jackets on because it felt almost as cold inside as it had outside. Resting on the floor, an old kerosene burner heated water in a well-used "Arabic" coffee pot into which he stirred dark, finely ground coffee. The five of us squatted in the customary manner around the warmth of the burner and smoked cigarettes while the coffee brewed. The room was filled with the harsh aroma of tobacco, and the rich aroma of coffee spiced with what I later learned was cardamom. We shared our cigarettes with our host, who seemed familiar with this brand that Israelis referred to as "forget-me-nots" because if you stopped puffing on them for too long, they'd extinguish.

After the coffee heated for a few minutes, he added a large amount of sugar to the pot, stirred it carefully, and served each of us a small cup that held an ounce or two of the intense brew. Our conversation was mostly in Hebrew, which he spoke very well as a second language. Some brief exchanges in Arabic occurred between him and two of our crew who were recent immigrants from one of the countries of North Africa—Morocco, if I remember correctly.

Squatting on the dirt floor, sipping hot, bittersweet coffee, I puffed on my cigarette and looked and listened. And while I did, the experience became powerful, even transformative—a variation of the "Jerusalem syndrome." In a way that I did not then nor do I now fully understand, it was as if I had lived there, belonged there, and had more in common with this elderly Palestinian man than I did with the other people in my life, including those I worked with in the bare wheat field on those several cold, overcast, damp days in the Galilee.

But there was something else. Close to sixty years have passed, and I'm still left with the same disturbing thought that had occurred to me after we had left the Galilee and returned to another life in the Jordan Valley. Had our gracious host, with whom I felt such a strong kinship, seen us as we had seen the other kind of enemies that occupied our land and devoured our crops?

The word "victim" remains at the heart of everyone's struggle in this land that people on both sides call "home." Palestinians feel displaced. And they have been, both within Israel and across the borders into neighboring states where many had no option but to settle in refugee camps. Israelis feel they are in the only place where Jews can be safe from centuries of persecution. History provides ample, supporting evidence.

The violence and hatred continues. Everyone a fish; everyone a jackal.

Living and working with Israeli Jews in 1963-64, I had limited contact with Palestinians. I could travel to places in Israel and, except in reference to the War of Independence and the Israeli victory, learn slightly more than nothing about the people that used to live on what became Israeli farmland, or villages, or towns, or cities.

I learned more about Roman ruins, and more recent ruins of buildings built by the British during the Mandate period, than I did about fifteen-year-old Palestinian ruins. In fact, I learned only years later that some of the ruins that I thought must have been Roman or British had been Palestinian homes and other structures, often built with the same ancient stones.

I returned to Israel twice, in 1966 for a few months and in 1978 for ten days. I'm now seventy-six and can't explain why I haven't been there since then. I do know that part of the explanation is that as the decades passed, and the Israel-Palestine conflict became more complex day after day, so did my attachment to the land.

~ ~ ~ ~ ~

Before it's too late, I'll be in Israel again, and will take all the time that is needed to be guided not only by the map I used in 1963 and 1964, but also by another map I will keep open by its side. Together, they will identify those places I had been but did not know were once Palestinian villages, farmland, towns, and neighborhoods.

My journey will end when I sit on the bank of the Sea of Galilee, where I so often was as a young man. There, I'll see the wonder I witnessed countless times and have visited in my thoughts countless times since: The sun will begin to set, the firmament and the face of the sea will turn their soft blues and pinks, and the Golan Heights will turn its dusty rose. And I will be filled with a sorrow as deep as the beauty before me, that we could not find the path to walk this sacred land together.

SEARCHING FOR THE ANCESTRAL CHURCH

Madison, Wisconsin, 1975. We had met a year earlier and discovered that both of us loved to walk—together. We walked through the numbing winter cold, in the spring when everything bloomed and all seemed possible, and in the early summer when we lingered under catalpa trees late at night as the flower petals fell around us in a soft, white veil. In the hot, mid-summer days and cooler evenings, we walked in the arboretum where, years earlier, Catherine had recorded the habits of wildlife, while remaining silent for hours. She had demonstrated this patience early in her life, and later nurtured it during her years in the convent as an aspirant.

With each walk, we grew more comfortable in our shared silences. I learned from her to honor those times when what is most important is listening to the sounds of the heart. And we held hands. And fell in love. I was thirty-two, Catherine was twenty-seven.

After twelve years of living together, we still shared our lives and household, but weren't yet married. One morning, we talked again of how vexatious, maybe impossible, it would be to find a rabbi and a priest to officiate at the wedding of this Jewish man and this Catholic woman. And we worried about something more important: what would we teach our children about religion, and could all of this become so overwhelming we might never move forward?

Silent once again, we stood close to each other as the sun streamed through the large window and appeared as a rectangle of sunlight on an unadorned white wall of our home. Catherine was the first to speak. There are times—and this would be one of them—when her words seem to echo a meditation or a prayer, something that might have been spoken best in Latin, in the convent, at Mass.

"It's upon us to understand how God manifests Himself."

Two small birds flew past the window, revealed only by their fleeting shadows crossing the sunlight on the wall.

"That's how God manifests Himself to me," I said.

"That's how He manifests Himself to me, too," Catherine said. "Let's *do* get married."

On the first afternoon of a three-day honeymoon on Sanibel Island, we purchased a belated wedding cake—one slice of key lime pie that we ate with plastic forks from a fine china paper plate. Our shoulders pressed together as we sat on a sun-bleached wooden bench under a shading palm tree in a park. To make the feast last longer, we took small bites that we fed to each other, making sure to capture the last crumbs of graham cracker and the last traces of whipping cream. These quiet acts confirmed our commitment, and evoked the words from the *Song of Solomon*, often recited by brides and grooms: "I am my beloved's; my beloved is mine."

It was the slow season, and we encountered but a small number of people, especially on the beach. The island's abundant array of seashells were always at their greatest number following a storm like the one that had preceded our visit. As we walked the long beach, we held hands, letting go when either of us spotted a special shell that called for close examination. At the ever-shifting margin of water and sand, new shells were exposed with each soft ebb and flow of a now calm sea.

A highway to Michigan, 2015. The road passes through an area where the gentle roll of the hills and their patchwork of farm fields, the abundance of birch, even the shapes of clouds announce we are no longer in southeast Wisconsin, in Milwaukee. We're on one of our many trips to visit family members in Catherine's birthplace, the Upper Peninsula of Michigan, where so much of importance to her has taken place.

"I feel as if I'm coming home," Catherine says to me, to herself, to those who are there and waiting, both the living and the departed. Meanwhile, I feel like "the other," an outsider, in the place where we're headed.

In 1897, her great-grandparents on her mother's side participated in a communal effort to lay the stone foundation of St. Bruno's Catholic Church in Nadeau. In nearby Daggett, her birthplace—population 248—St. Frederick's would have remained ancestral on her father's side of the family, but the parish was merged with another parish in the 1980s. Now, the old church building is a private home. Most of the parishioners worship four miles away in Stephenson, where the Church of the Precious Blood acquired a measure of ancestral status when Catherine's father's parents were married there one hundred years ago.

Close to Precious Blood is the township cemetery where many members of three generations of her extended family are buried in a layer of rich, black topsoil. Her parents lie side by side at the edge of the cemetery under an aged apple tree, a living monument rivaling others carved from granite. With its few remaining, crooked limbs, the tree stands, a resolute sentinel, overlooking bucolic fields and woods in peaceful in shades of spring and summer green, the blazing red and gold of autumn, and the pristine snow-white of long, Upper Peninsula winters.

During the Christmas season, as a way of capturing something of the ancestral church embrace, Catherine arranges a crèche on a living room table in our home. The figures and objects are clay representations, without refined features, hand-shaped in a Mexican village, and painted in the rich hues favored by local tradition. Mary and Joseph watch over the manger that holds baby Jesus. Close to them is a cluster of clay sheep, ducks, and two other children, one of whom carries a bouquet of red flowers, the other a white chicken. To complete the scene, Catherine adds a couple dozen hand-carved wooden animals, none more than an inch long, some less than half that. These witnesses of the blessed event are extended families of rabbits, chipmunks, squirrels, raccoons, skunks, and a single fawn without its parents.

In years when the solar Gregorian calendar, and the lunar Jewish calendar bring Christmas and Chanukah together, we do the same. A *menorah* sits near the crèche to honor the important holiday of my own religion. Yet, for me, it's the crèche that feels more accessible. Like the end of Mass. Offer your neighbors your hand and accept theirs.

Peace be with you. Feel it in your heart. As Catherine feels about the ancestral church, and her birthplace, where many of her relatives still raise their children, work, pray, grow old, and expect to be buried.

Deep as my thoughts are about Catherine, when we enter Marinette and approach the Menominee River Bridge to Michigan, what has happened before happens again. My grip tightens on the steering wheel as one or another painful memories return. I'm never certain which one it will be: the girlfriend's parents who didn't want their daughter to date a Jew; the man who insisted that Jews stole milk from the German Christians who then could not feed their babies? No, this time it's the snowstorm.

It snowed hard that day in 1959, when I was sixteen. My family lived on a street with a moderate incline to the top of the hill. From the sidewalk, I watched a large sedan lose all traction and stop. I walked into the street and, through the closed side window, said to the driver that I could help her. She stomped on the gas pedal, and the tires screamed on the compacted snow. Then, the rear brake lights shone bright red when she must have stomped her foot on the pedal. She rolled down the window a few inches and said, "I don't need help from a Jew," and pressed hard on the door lock button. Beyond infuriated, I said, "I'm going to find one of my baseball bats and smash your lights and windows." An African American custodian for several of the apartment buildings walked toward us. He and I always said hello when we saw each other. This time, he said, "Under control," making a "calm down" motion with both hands in front of him. I nodded and walked to the sidewalk. The driver

moved to the passenger side of the front bench seat, he took her
place at the steering wheel, and they drove with ease to the top
of the hill.

"I'm probably the only Jew your relatives know," I say to
Catherine, and to myself.

Her response has happened before, and happens again.
"You know that's not true. You know my grandmother's
brother, Joe, married a Jew, and my cousin married a woman
whose father is Jewish. And you know about Mr. Cohen
who bought cattle from the farmers. Remember? He'd stay
overnight with the family when my mother and her brothers
and sister were children? He said he could trust a family who
prayed together."

"Right. I remember all of that, Cathy, but I still feel
alone when we cross the bridge."

I loosen the grip of my right hand on the steering wheel
and reach to touch Catherine's arm, knowing she'll help me
through this, as she always does. I'm that toddler who runs
from a playgroup, touches the arm or leg of his parent, feels
safe, and runs off again.

"I don't feel alone," she says, "but I do feel a longing
for how I used to be enveloped in family and religion. It all
came together, but not now, at least not in the same way.
Now, there are times I long for what I've lost."

"Which is . . . ?"

"When I'm in church, the *true* faith that was in my heart
when I was younger is still there, but I don't feel the same
about the *institution* of the Church."

"I don't long for anything like that, or even an ancestral

synagogue like what I think of as your ancestral church. Honestly, if I have one at all, it's eight time zones to the east, in the hills of Jerusalem or by the Sea of Galilee."

This would be another of those times when Catherine speaks of faith, lost or found, and her words become more formal, more devout. "You and I found a different way that works for us. We built our own family . . . we brought love to it. And kindness. In that way, the Church is within us. That's what feels true."

I'm captivated by her words. As we continue north toward her family, there is nothing more we need to say. I reach to touch her arm just as she reaches to touch mine; our hands meet, and remain together for a few tenths of a mile. Sheltered, not alone, each knows that the other shares the same search. And it unites us, as it always has.

PART V

Unanswerable Questions

Under the harvest moon,
When the soft silver
Drips shimmering
Over the garden nights,
Death, the gray mocker,
Comes and whispers to you
As a beautiful friend
Who remembers.

Under the summer roses
When the flagrant crimson
Lurks in the dusk
Of the wild red leaves,
Love, with little hands,
Comes and touches you
With a thousand memories,
And asks you
Beautiful, unanswerable questions.

–Carl Sandburg, "Under the Harvest Moon"

BUT ONE MOURNFUL CHORD

In the last week of September 1955, the extended family was told that twenty minutes before the shot was fired, my mother's brother, Uncle Hymie, had called home to ask if he should bring anything from the market where he worked—anything, that is, in addition to the pistol he'd been cleaning in the office.

Aunt Edith, Hymie's wife, explained to their two daughters that there had been a robbery near their apartment, and the pistol their father had been cleaning would provide protection, if needed. Everyone else in the family was told the same. Elders offered the timing and content of the phone call as evidence that the death had been accidental: Why would he have called home to ask if he should bring anything from the market if he intended to kill himself right then?

In an attempt to have this interpretation become official, my father hired an attorney whose influence with the coroner could be helpful at the inquest. In addition to a few important practical matters that usually accompany the death of a parent with survivors, the reputation of my uncle's family made it desirable for the coroner to rule the death an accident, which he did. The report stated the pistol was defective and had backfired.

At the age of twelve, I harbored thoughts too uncomfortable to ask out loud. Were the elders protecting us from the truth? Had there even been a phone call? Would my uncle have been cleaning a loaded pistol? Did he shoot himself in the chest, as we were told? I thought people shot themselves in the head when committing suicide, but I figured my uncle might have decided it was less frightening to fire into his chest. I had the questions, but no answers that made sense to me.

Neither the assurances by family members nor the coroner's report could prevent rumors from surfacing in the community, as I learned the hard way when a grade school classmate approached me on the playground after the funeral.

"My parents said your uncle committed suicide."

"I don't . . . I don't think so," I said, not knowing what to believe.

More than sixty years later, I still don't know what to believe. The cloud of uncertainty that had formed in the first minutes after my dying uncle had been discovered, quickly descended as fog. The decades that followed were marked by silence, faded or repressed memories, and then the deaths of two generations of elders—our grandparents and parents.

~ ~ ~ ~ ~

As did thousands of Polish Jews, Isadore and Tillie Faier immigrated to America: Isadore in 1911, Tillie following a year later. Destined to become my grandparents, they settled in a neighborhood of St. Louis that had become home to European Jews. There they established I. Faier's

Kosher Delicatessen. Impoverished scholars, writers, and poets were among the many customers they sheltered there, some writing at the small tables and some relying upon my grandmother to slip them sandwiches.

Three children were born to them: Hyman (Hymie) in 1914, my mother, Sylvia (Surelah), in 1916, and Anita (Butsie) in 1924. As the three children became old enough, each had special jobs to do, among sundry other chores. This became the focus of conversation when my wife and I enjoyed one of our last visits with Aunt Butsie before she died in 2011.

When we arrived at her and my uncle's house for breakfast, we saw just how ill she was. All of us knew she didn't have long to live, yet she looked so serene and lovely, though thin and tired. We finished our meal, and my aunt walked to the kitchen. We heard a drawer open and close, and then she returned to the table.

"I have something for you," she said to me. "This was your grandfather's, and now you and Catherine should have it."

She unwrapped two layers of newspaper that had been protecting a fifteen-inch butcher's knife. Holding it flat in both hands, she presented it. The knife felt crafted for my hand. Its wood handle was marked with small abrasions and dings from years of use. The blade, fashioned for slicing, had a gentle curve and widened from handle to tip.

"It's still sharp. Did I ever tell you the story about the knives?" Aunt Butsie said. "No? Well, now I will. Even when we were very young, your mother, Hymie, and I had jobs in the delicatessen. Hymie, of course, continued working there as an adult until your grandparents retired and closed the delicatessen. My job was to make sure the knives that needed it got to the sharpener. You remember electric streetcars, don't you? One of them ran down the center of the avenue, and there was a stop near the delicatessen. I'd wrap the knives in paper and wait to give the package to the conductor, Pop would call the sharpener to let him know the knives were on their way, the sharpener would wait at his stop, the conductor would give him the knives, and when he finished his work, he'd call your grandfather. That's how I would know when to meet the streetcar again at our stop. That's how we did it. That was my job."

She looked so proud, so happy to share with us this memory of childhood. Her story brought to life the delicatessen and the early years of our family more than any other story I could remember. And it added another layer of poignancy to a particular photograph I had seen many times before in an album my mother had given me shortly before she died in 2001.

In that 1916 photograph, Isadore Faier stands in the delicatessen doorway, dressed in his dark suit pants, vest, white shirt, and tie. His sleeves are rolled to just below the elbow. Next to him stands his firstborn, his son, two-year-old Hymie, whose head does not reach the top of his father's thigh. They pose holding hands, as my grandmother, Tillie, watches over them from a second-floor window. The proud parents would not have imagined their son would precede them in death.

Several years after the end of World War II, my grandparents retired, but I. Faier's remained a gold standard for the next generation of St. Louis kosher delicatessens. Whenever a new proprietor asked for my grandfather's advice, he gave it. Several of these men told me how much they appreciated my grandfather's assistance, and how much they owed him for his generosity and wisdom.

To this day, I feel a grandson's pride when I recall these stories. But, I also have a deep sense of regret, and a measure of resentment, that these men had enjoyed what I had wanted, but never received: the attention of my grandfather. He and I didn't have what could be called a "relationship," though we were often in each other's company. He remained remote to me throughout his life; I can't remember having a conversation with him, even when I was a teenager, no longer the little boy at the dinner table.

Nevertheless, I do have indelible memories of him seated at the head of the table, flanked by family, as he presided over the rituals of Sabbath and other holidays. I remember being with him a few times as our family worshipped together in the synagogue. In the photo album given to me by my mother, I see my grandfather in conservative suits, often double-breasted, well-tailored for his medium height and slender physique. When he appears in his topcoat, it sometimes is accented by one of several silk scarves, also given to me by my mother. My grandfather's black mustache, graying as he ages, is always neatly trimmed. His face has a certain delicacy that speaks of sensitivity and thoughtfulness. I see him holding a granddaughter on his lap, and his loving smile conveys an unmistakable softness and sweetness.

On many Sundays, when I was a young boy, my father took my grandfather on drives through the countryside outside of St. Louis. I don't recall that my grandmother or my mother joined those excursions, but usually one or both of my brothers and I did. From my usual place in the back seat, I could see my grandfather's shoulders and the side of his face. Years later, we would sit in the same relationship to each other, he in front, I behind him, though not in an automobile.

On a day in the last week of September 1955, when I was twelve, I walked into our apartment, and my fifteen-year-old brother met me in the hallway.

"Uncle Hymie had an accident," he said with a somber voice and face, "and he died. All we know right now is he shot himself."

Shot himself? What does that mean? A bewildered twelve-year-old with little comprehension of how profound this event was, and would remain, I didn't know what to do but lie facedown on my bed and cry.

At the time of Uncle Hymie's death in 1955, I. Faier's Kosher Delicatessen had been closed for at least seven years, during which my uncle had taken the opportunity to join his father-in-law's seafood business. Soon thereafter, my grandfather arranged to use a small space in their business to sell traditional delicatessen items . . . and once again to work near his son.

The business was located in a public market on the first floor of a multi-story, brick building in downtown St. Louis. The market provided offices in the basement, so it wasn't out of the ordinary that my uncle had gone downstairs; but when he didn't return, his relatives became concerned. Large masonry pillars, thick walls, and the commotion of a busy market made it impossible for anyone upstairs to have heard the shot.

I've never been certain who was the first to descend the steps and discover my uncle, mortally wounded. Was it his father? His father-in-law? The two people who might have known said to me they didn't remember. My own memory is that several years after her brother died, my mother told me that as he lay dying on the office floor, he said to his father, my grandfather, "Pop, help me." In the way that was so familiar to me, she tilted her head and gave a tender smile . . . either to me, as I hoped, or to someone in the distance where her gaze seemed to rest. I wanted to console her, but didn't have the words.

What I think of as "Death in the Market" remains for me as two scenes on a split screen. There is the 1916 photograph of my proud grandfather holding the hand of his two-year-old son as they pose in the doorway of the delicatessen. And there is the other scene of my helpless grandfather holding the hand of the forty-one-year-old son whose life ebbs as he bleeds in a basement office of a public market, while the crowd upstairs continues to buy and sell, unaware of the drama unfolding below them.

The funeral was the first I attended. Trying to fathom what was happening around me, I wandered through the unfamiliar environment of the funeral home, watching and listening. I moved closer to a small group and heard a mourner say, "It's a terrible thing when a son buries his father, but when a father has to bury his son . . ." She raised her hands, palms open, as if she were hoping to find in the very air around her a tolerable way to finish the awful thought. At a number of places in the funeral home and chapel, I heard muffled weeping and unsettling sobs from more than one mourner. One woman slumped against another to keep from collapsing.

In the chapel, the funeral directors had placed a tray of small glass capsules, each wrapped in a tight layer of white gauze. To find something that might help a twelve-year-old fathom what was happening in that chapel and to my family, I imitated the few older mourners who crushed the capsules and held them to their noses. The gauze wrapping protected my fingers, as it was intended to do; but when I held the capsule under my nose and breathed in, as I saw others doing, it released shocking fumes of ammonia that penetrated deep into my sinuses. It felt like the fumes filled my entire skull, and I shook my head rapidly from side to side to clear it.

I was thankful when the service finally began. My grandfather sat in the first-row pew with my grandmother, my mother and Butsie, and Hymie's widow and two fatherless daughters. Just as I had done in the car on our Sunday excursions, I sat behind my grandfather. Every few moments, his shoulders raised and lowered and a soft and rhythmic sound emanated from what seemed to be his entire body, an instrument that played but one mournful chord.

Then, he would compose himself until, once again, he could not contain his wordless grief. Each time I saw his shoulders move and heard that rhythmic sound, for an instant I thought he was laughing. Each time, I felt ashamed to have misunderstood, and thankful no one could have read my thoughts.

In spite of the tragedy, in the months that followed, there was a measure of healing. I. Faier's Kosher Delicatessen made a curtain call in 1956, a year after my uncle's death. His widow opened a new establishment, Faier's Delicatessen, which would serve its customers for the next twelve years. My grandfather again had the opportunity to share his wealth of knowledge and, on many days, to assist behind the counter. On numerous visits, I watched him operate the slicing machine with a swift precision that came from years of practice. His working there might have been comforting to him, but it also would have required great strength. But that strength would not last much longer.

February 1960. Isadore Faier's heart stopped beating. In truth, it had begun to fail on that day in the market, five years earlier. We waited for our father to come home from the hospital where my grandfather had been rushed. When he entered the front hallway, I was standing in the same spot where I had been standing when I'd learned of my uncle's death.

"Grandpa died," were my father's kind words. And they were enough.

At the funeral, prayers were intoned and eulogies delivered in the chapel where they had been intoned and delivered for his son. This time, at age seventeen, I was a pallbearer. Compared to his son's death, my grandfather's felt more "normal" and was more understandable. But much about it still eluded me, a proud young adult only approaching manhood. In my still-young eyes, when my grandfather died, he was an old man. I smile now at my naiveté. He had lived but seventy-three years, two years fewer than I have as I write these words.

The procession arrived at the cemetery on a day that seemed without a breath of wind. Cotton snowflakes began their gentle fall and melted as they touched the ground. The brief snowfall imparted a softness to bare trees and row after row of chiseled granite headstones. The graveside service for my grandfather began under a canopy where mourners gathered for prayer. We stood only a short distance from the grave of my grandfather's son.

Sixty-three years have passed since my uncle died, and I'm now the father of two adult children whom I love with boundless joy and devotion. For that reason, far more than any other, I empathize with my grandfather's anguish in ways I could not have done before becoming a parent. My uncle's death had violated the natural order. Children are not to die before their parents.

No longer is my grandfather merely the remote elder, two generations removed from me. He also is a father, as am I. We have at least this part of a "relationship." I do wish we were able to meet again now that there is something we might be able to build upon . . . something far more important to me than silk scarves and a knife from I. Faier's Kosher Delicatessen.

I often think of my grandfather sitting in front of me on that pew in the funeral chapel. Perchance, in his despair, he would have recalled, as I do now, those words of King David:

O my son Absalom, my son Absalom! Would God I had died for thee, O Absalom, my son, my son!

SWEET BLINTZES

Prologue, *circa* 1951, age 8

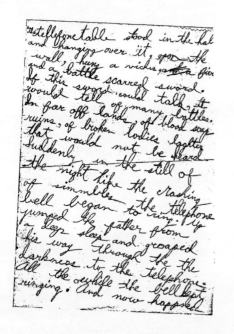
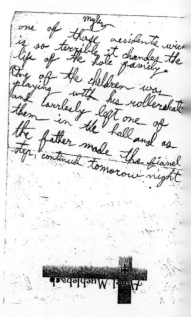

Tomorrow night, sixty-seven years later. "You always, always were Grandma's favorite," one cousin says. Another says, with wonder, "What can you even say about it?" and hears in response, "Why even try?"

They might not know what to say, but I do. It's simple.

From the time I was a toddler, I have enjoyed the exalted status of "Our Grandmother's Favorite." As some might imagine an angel would have done, for the remainder of her life, my mother's mother provided the protection and unconditional love she must have sensed I needed. She must have been aware of my young sorrow. I felt this from the touch of her hand, from her smile when she held me, from how pleased she was as I devoured as many as I could of her sweet, cheese-filled blintzes with golden raisins and sprinkled with just the right amount of cinnamon and sugar. These delicacies were food for my soul, long before I could have understood the meaning of those words.

The tradition of observing Sabbath and other holidays at our grandparents' apartment began even before their three children had made them grandparents. The first two grandchildren arrived in 1940; by 1955, we were a group of eight, "the cousins." At or near the end of a meal or prayers, any of us old enough to walk would sometimes leave the table and watch television on the living room Philco. Housed within a mahogany-colored wooden cabinet with two doors that swung to either side, its small screen was shaped like the icon still used when an advertisement announces, "As seen on TV!" On some of the Friday evenings, we watched prizefights sponsored by Gillette, the company that could make a man "look sharp, feel sharp, be sharp."

When the fight was an important one, some of the adults would wander from the dining table and through the wide arch into the living room.

My grandmother's favorite chair was positioned a few

feet from the Philco. The prizefights were not her top show. That spot was reserved for professional wrestling. All of us who watched with her were ardent fans of the Champion, Lou Thesz. We reviled the challenger, Gorgeous George, who, in fact, wasn't gorgeous, with his bleached-blond hair and tight, white swimming suit. We grandchildren tried to convince our grandmother that the matches were rigged. By her reaction, you would have thought we had told her that Jews observe Sabbath on Sunday, heaven forfend.

These meals and celebrations continued, but on a less frequent basis as the cousins became interested in other things, like boyfriends, girlfriends, parties, and sporting events. When our grandfather died in February 1960, what had been known as "being at our grandparents' apartment" did not take long to end.

By the following fall and early winter, our grandmother's physical and mental health had deteriorated enough that she had begun to find it very difficult to live alone. At my parents' insistence, she moved into our apartment. I was in my first year of college, not close enough to home for me to visit other than during summer or other school breaks.

My parents had moved the Philco, along with her favorite chair, into Grandma's new bedroom. Failing eyesight now required her to be close enough to the television screen to touch it. Whenever I was at home, I would pull up a chair and watch with her and Iris Banks, now Grandma's caregiver, who would sit at her side.

Divorce Court had replaced professional wrestling as Grandma's top show. If the plaintiff or defendant—whichever was their favorite that day—experienced a setback, Iris would shake her head, commenting, "That judge!" or "They lied." Grandma would put her hand to her cheek and use the Yiddish *"Oy!"* when the situation was bad, *"Oy vey!"* when the situation was worse, and *"Vey ist mir!* Woe is me!" when it threatened to be a disaster. I had learned from years of enjoying professional wrestling not to say, "Grandma, don't worry. This isn't real." On the rare occasion when my impulse control failed, it was difficult to determine who was more irritated with me—Grandma or Iris.

But, it wasn't difficult to know that Grandma was upset and worried when she thought I might do something she believed would have dire consequences. In the summer of 1961, I was hired by a construction company in St. Louis. I sat with her in her room and told her about the job. Not more than a couple seconds had passed before she said in a soft, almost conspiratorial voice, "Listen, my *shepsela*, my dear one. Come close." She rested her hand on my arm. "You must not take this job."

"Why, Grandma?" I said, moving even closer to her.

"You must not."

"But why not?"

"It isn't good for you."

"Grandma . . . it's not the kind of construction job you think it is. I'll be in the office most of the time, keeping records for the foreman." Certain that her concern was for my safety, I reassured her. "Don't worry, Grandma. I promise it won't be dangerous."

"No, you must not." She accompanied this with a gentle squeeze of her hand where she had rested it on my arm. "What will happen when people drive down the highway and they see you and say, '*Oy vey*. Look. It's Sylvia Hopper's son working on the highway!'"

Her hand still on my arm, I said something that I should have anticipated would have the same persuasive power for Grandma as would a villainous *Divorce Court* attorney arguing with the judge, or Gorgeous George arguing with the referee. "Grandma, I promise you have nothing to worry about. I won't be on the highway. I'll be in an office."

"*Sha*. Listen to me," she said, emphasizing it with another squeeze of my arm, this time a bit tighter than the first. "You don't know. I know. It vill *happen*."

I did keep my job. Had "it" happened, my grandmother wouldn't have blamed me. The driver would have been blamed for spying on other people's family members instead of paying attention to the road. Nevertheless, at the construction site, I was careful not to stand anywhere where people driving by might recognize me as Sylvia Hopper's son.

The next winter. When I was nineteen, during the holiday break from college, it snowed in St. Louis. One evening, my fifteen-year-old brother and I threw snowballs at lampposts, parked cars, an occasional moving car, and anything else that seemed, at least to me, like an appropriate target, such as my brother. When I did nothing more than hit him in the head with a perfect shot that might have hurt him, he was infuriated, and rushed up the steps to our apartment. I walked after him.

Our mother stood in the dining room, hovering, as she often did, at the periphery of an unfolding scene that had potential for conflict between my father and me. Grandma was at the Formica and aluminum kitchen table, and motioned to me to sit across from her. No doubt as a means of coping with my own anxiety, I focused my attention on the ingenious way this table could store a wing underneath each side of the tabletop and extend them to make the table larger. I noticed that toast crumbs had searched for and settled in their favorite place: the narrow gaps between the wings and tabletop.

My father walked down the hall with quick, heavy footsteps. Wearing his comfortable khakis and a white T-shirt, he arrived at the kitchen and stood with his hands pressed against both sides of the doorframe, his feet planted in a wide stance. The wings of the table and the toast crumbs were no longer of concern to me. My father's stance was not unlike the depiction of Samson dislodging the two central pillars to collapse the temple of the Philistines.

"What did you do?" he said.

"I threw a snowball, and it hit him in the head."

"I already know that."

Grandma was sitting between my father and me and had turned in her chair to look straight at him. "Well, if you already know it, why are you asking me?" I said, taunting him.

I felt safe. All three of us understood Grandma, my protector, was there to shield me. I understood that my father would never want to do anything to upset her, but I was afraid he wouldn't be able to control his anger. I was afraid he wouldn't remember a promise I had made to him two years earlier, in this same kitchen. This was the confrontation I had told Nick about when we two gray-haired men had sat in his office comparing notes about our fathers. I was seventeen, not a boy any longer, but still frightened. "I don't give a shit how you feel about it," I had said, and stood several feet from him. "You will never hit me again." And he never again did. The fear never vanished; it subsided year by year, until I was able to put it back into its box and close tight the lid, though it sometimes forced its way out, into the light, like tonight.

"Why would you do that to your brother?" he said.

"All I did was bean him, but he's not hurt."

"Can't we have peace around here?" This was less a question than a demand, and I had the old feeling that this situation would deteriorate. "Okay. That's it," he said, removing his hands from both sides of the doorframe. "Stop the damned grinning. You sit here grinning like you don't even care."

"*Sha!*" my grandmother said. "Vhat are you saying? He's not grinning. Leave him alone. I'm sitting vith him, and you yell at him to stop grinning and he isn't grinning. You should not say this."

My father lifted his hands to heaven—an act that had been perfected by everyone in our family—and retreated down the hallway.

When she was sure my father was too far from us to hear what she was about to say, my grandmother leaned across the kitchen table and took my hand in both of hers.

"*Nu? Vell?*" she said, almost in a whisper. "So vhat means grinning?"

In the months that followed, it had become more apparent that Grandma was losing her strength, even her will to live. One of the last times I was with her, in the summer of 1963, eighteen months after the kitchen scene, she sat at the dining room table with my mother, father, younger brother, and me. Despondent, she wouldn't eat.

"Grandma, you have to eat," I said.

She looked down as she shook her head, "No, I can't."

"Please, Grandma."

She lifted her fork a few inches, then let her hand fall to the table. "I can't lift the fork."

"It's okay, Grandma. I won't eat, either."

"Eat. You must. Don't wait for me."

"If you don't eat, I don't eat." I lowered my fork onto the plate.

She reached for her fork, took some food from her plate, and began to eat, thereby ensuring that my status of favorite grandchild would remain secure, no doubt forever . . . and everyone at the table knew it.

Later that year, our family had become pushpins on a map of the world. My older brother and his wife and daughter already were living in England, where he was teaching and completing graduate school; my younger brother had begun a year as a high school exchange student in South Africa; and I was in Israel, living in the kibbutz in the Jordan Valley. Our parents and our grandmother remained in St. Louis.

In that year when all three boys were gone, there were occasions to grieve: My father grieved that his sons had left, and nothing would ever be the same; my mother grieved for the same reasons; Grandma grieved over the loss of so many of her family, first in Poland and then in America; and I grieved over saying what I believed would be a final farewell to the person who treated me as her favorite grandchild.

February 1964. At the end of a long workday in the kibbutz fishponds, I walked toward the wooden cabin I called home. The community mailman sped down the path on his bicycle, his preferred method of delivering the mail. He skidded to a stop, and handed me a very thin envelope. I didn't need to check the return address. I recognized my father's distinct handwriting.

The other letters I had received from him or my mother had been thicker than this one, so I had a premonition that I wouldn't like what I was about to read. I sat on the cabin porch and read the few simple and kind words he had written. More times than I can remember, I reread, "Your grandmother died peacefully, among family, having lived a good and happy life."

Holding my father's letter, somehow I was able to go beyond myself, to feel as much sorrow for his loss as for my own. I didn't know at the time all that I was to learn only a few years later about his adoption and the truth about his biological mother. But, I understood that he had just lost a woman he loved, much as he had loved his own mother who had suffered before she died from cancer in 1937. When he lost his mother, he had been only three years older than I was when he mailed me the letter about Grandma's death. I have no doubt that as he wrote, he had already said the *Kaddish*— the prayer in memory of the departed—numerous times for his mother-in-law, and had included his mother, Minnie, and his father, Saul.

Fifty-four annual calendars have been taken down from the wall and replaced since I was that young man on the cabin porch. Thirty-three of those calendars have been replaced since my father's death. I have needed all of that time to understand that the moments of reading his letter had been a critical part of my long emergence from having felt suspended like a bead threaded on a string stretched taut between two poles, represented by *Grandmother* and *Father*. Beyond doubt, one was safe, tender, and clarifying, while at any given moment the other could be dangerous, harsh, and confusing.

If I were to write to that young man, age twenty-one, I would try to find my own simple and kind words to tell him that one day he will know that he has become a gentle and loving father. He will know that in spite of what is his persistent struggle with all that has been damaging, he also carries within himself all that was good in his own father.

When I think of my grandmother and her sweet, soul-nourishing blintzes, of my father and his many acts of kindness that far outnumbered his moments of rage, and of myself, both as that young man and who he has become, the same thing happens. I hear myself saying, "Don't worry, Grandma. I'm safe."

REMEMBERING KEN KESEY

Summer 2012. The four of us were savoring ravioli stuffed with wild mushrooms and a mixed salad with ginger dressing and topped with grilled salmon. My wife and I had met another couple at a favorite restaurant on what happened to be the fifty-year anniversary of the debut of Ken Kesey's *One Flew Over the Cuckoo's Nest.* We began to talk about the book.

A man and woman in their mid-twenties sat at the next table. "Oh my God! You're talking about my favorite author," the woman said.

One of our dinner companions nodded in my direction and said, "He spent time with him back in the sixties."

"You're totally kidding."

"No, he isn't," I said.

"Wow. That's amazing."

With that, all of us returned to our separate conversations and what was left of our meals.

Spring 1965. In my final year as an undergraduate, Ken Kesey had accepted an invitation to travel from the West Coast to speak at our college and meet with students. I was the lucky one who picked him up at the bus station.

During the short drive to the college in my Beetle, sporting a large orange flower decal hiding a dent on the driver's door, I said to him, "I was surprised to learn you were taking the bus. I thought I'd be driving to the airport."

"I don't like to fly," he said. "On the bus, I have a chance to hear what the other passengers are talking about." He removed a pen and spiral notepad from his shirt pocket and wrote a few lines. "When I hear something I think fits my characters' dialogue, I write it down."

Later in the day, in one of his informal sessions with a group of about ten of us, Mr. Kesey talked about his writing and his sense of the absurdity of existence. This appealed to most of us in the room. It was hip (in one vernacular of the mid-sixties) to reveal your existential angst. Young men (such as I) accentuated this by wearing sport jackets with holes at the elbows, not patched by leather ovals. For maximum effect, it was *de rigueur* to need a haircut, and carry a book (something "really deep") tall enough to peek out of the jacket pocket so everyone would be impressed by the carrier's serious commitment to becoming an intellectual. Young women had at least one sweater with holes (or about-to-be holes) in the elbows, carried "really deep" books in well-worn canvas or leather shoulder bags, and (if genes permitted) wore their long hair straight (ironing hair on the ironing board acceptable), parted in the center, no barrettes, God forbid.

It was hard for me to resist asking our guest something I thought might be received as unwelcome, even provocative; since he'd opened the door by inviting us to ask anything we wanted, I chose to walk right in.

"Mr. Kesey, I have a question. You've talked about how absurd or meaningless life is." I paused. Breathed. "Well, if you actually believe this, why haven't you killed yourself?"

If a question can have physical substance, this one did. It was like a block of rough stone falling from the sky and landing in the middle of a happy family's picnic blanket. The room was filled with an awkward silence of about four or five seconds—that felt like four or five hours—until I couldn't bear it.

"I'm sorry if I offended you," I said.

"No, no. That's a good question. I have an answer for you. Here's what it's all about for me. Our family was in the kitchen, and our son, not a year old, was in his high chair. I was on the other side of the room and saw him stand up, and knew he was going to fall headfirst onto the floor." He paused for a few seconds. There was no sound that I remember, not even a shuffling of shoes or a cough. He continued. "I ran and caught him before his little head would have hit. I didn't think. Because of my love for my son, I just acted. That's my whole answer."

He hadn't altered his relaxed posture in the chair, or his calm manner of talking to us. Compared to how apprehensive I had been that I might experience his anger or resentment, his soft-spoken answer was a relief. This considerate man is wonderful, I concluded. He could have embarrassed me in front of everyone in the room, and I might have deserved it.

"I really appreciate that you answered the question," I said. "It's an answer I can . . . I mean . . . it makes perfect sense to me. I feel the same way."

Nothing else about that session or the rest of Mr. Kesey's

visit has stuck with me—not even whether I had returned him to the bus station. I like to think I did, and that we talked all the way there, and after I dropped him off, I saw in the rearview mirror that he was writing in his notebook every stunning word I had spoken during his entire visit.

Winter 1984. Too few years after that visit to our college and his answer to my youthful question, Ken Kesey is unable to run across a room, or any other space, to catch his son before his head hit the floor—or anything else.

> UPI, SPOKANE, Wash., Jan. 23. Jed Kesey, the 20-year-old son of the author Ken Kesey, died today of injuries suffered in an accident on an icy road . . . when a van carrying the [wrestling] team skidded Saturday near Pomeroy in southeastern Washington . . .

Soon after his son's funeral, the grieving father composes a letter to five friends.

> . . . Partners . . . indulge me a little; I am but hurt . . . We built the box ourselves . . . and Zane and Jed's friends and frat brothers dug the hole in a nice spot between the chicken house and the pond . . . About 300 people stood around . . . While we were singing "Blue Eyes Crying in the Rain," Zane and Kit and the neighbor boys that have grown up with all of us carried the box to the hole.

Then, he writes about the nails, the burial, and the dirt.

> . . . [T]he boys each hammered in the one nail they
> had remembered to put in their pockets . . . and
> lowered the box . . . Zane and I tossed in the first
> shovelfuls. It sounded like the first thunderclaps
> of Revelations.

Then, he returns to the final moments of his son's life.

> . . . [At] the hospital . . . Zane and I had been
> carrying plastic bags of snow to pack his head in
> trying to stop the swelling . . . as blood poured
> to the bruised brain . . . [E]verybody had been
> exhorting him to "Hang on, Old Timer." . . .
> "Sure it hurts but you can pull through it." . . .
> And then aw by Jesus, we saw it in his face. The
> peacefully swollen un-conscious blank suddenly
> was filled with expression. He came back in . . .
> and he saw better than we could begin to imagine
> how terribly hurt he was. His poor face grimaced
> with pain . . . And then, O my old buddies, he
> cried.

But what he writes next grips me with such force that
I experience some small part of the ache in the heart of
another father.

> The doctors had already told us in every gentle
> way they could that he was brain dead, gone for

good, but we all saw it . . . the quick flickerback of consciousness, the awful hurt being realized, the tears saying "I don't think I can do 'er this time, Dad. I'm sorry, I truly am . . ."

Then, a final, awful decision.

. . . [Later, t]he phone rang in the nurses' quarters. It was the doctor . . . "Your son is essentially dead, Mr. Kesey. I'm very sorry." . . . Then the doctor . . . said he was wondering how Jed would have felt about being an organ donor . . .

"He would love it! . . . Take whatever you can use!" The doctor . . . told us that to take the kidneys they had to take them before the life support was turned off . . .

So Faye and I had to sign five copies apiece . . . while the machine pumped out the little beep . . . beep . . . beep . . . In all my life, waking and dreaming, I've never imagined anything harder . . .

We've heard since that they used twelve things out of him, including corneas. And the redwinged blackbirds sing in the budding greengage plumtree.

With love,
Ken

P.S. When Jed's wallet was finally sorted out of the
debris and confusion of the wreck it was discovered
that he had . . . signed the place on his driver's license
indicating that he wanted to be an organ donor . . .
One man gathers what another man spills. From:
Remembering Jed Kesey, in *CoEvolution Quarterly*,
1984, and elsewhere.

Summer 2019. Though Ken Kesey has been dead for
eighteen years, every time I read his letter, I imagine asking
him, "After the death of your son, how did you manage to
take your first step as a survivor?" I think of this question as a
sad sequel to the one I had asked him fifty years earlier about
the absurdity of life, and why he chose to continue living.

His answer to my imagined question is found in his
actions: he reached to touch others, as he once had reached
to catch his infant son; he reached to complete strangers
with his spontaneous, "He would love it," when asked
about organ donation; he reached to hundreds who were
welcomed to Jed's funeral; and he no doubt comforted
five of his closest friends with his letter of such tender and
sorrowful beauty, even while asking of them to " . . . indulge
me a little; I am but hurt."

I imagine saying to Mr. Kesey, once again, "I really
appreciate that you answered the question. It's an answer I
can . . . I mean . . . it makes perfect sense to me." But this time,
I don't add, "I feel the same way," because I can't imagine it.

A few weeks ago, I agree to meet a friend for lunch at the "Oh my God! You're talking about my favorite author" restaurant. Since I'm ten minutes early, I wait for him at a table and can't help but begin to fantasize about what would happen if the young couple and I were to meet here again. It doesn't take long for the fantasy to take shape.

A young woman approaches and says, "I thought I recognized you. You're the one who met Ken Kesey. Do you remember me?"

"I sure do. I actually had wanted to tell you the story, but with all of us eating dinner, it wasn't the right time." I ask if she would like to hear it now.

"Totally," she says and waves to her boyfriend who brings their after-lunch espressos with little cookies perched on the saucers, and the two of them sit down. I tell her about my time with Mr. Kesey in 1965, my question, and his answer. She says she's envious because he's still her favorite author.

I hesitate for a moment, but decide to ask her, "Do you know about his son?"

She raises her eyebrows and lowers her demitasse onto its saucer, causing only the faintest clink of porcelain on porcelain. "No . . . I don't."

At this moment, she's as young and vulnerable as I had been in 1965 when I met Mr. Kesey at the train station. Her apprehension is so apparent I want to be sure to treat her as thoughtfully and sensitively as her favorite author had treated me. I want to ease into the story, so I take a moment to have a sip of water.

"You need to know this is a difficult story." I wait for her to have a chance to respond, but she doesn't. So, I begin.

"It was on an icy road . . ."

LIFE AND DEATH ON THE ISLAND

Fred was my best native Newfoundlander friend when I lived in the Province of Newfoundland and Labrador for three and a half years, beginning in late summer of 1971. Both of us were employed at Memorial University in the provincial capital, St. John's, where Fred was a social worker, I was an anthropologist, and we were faculty colleagues in the Social Work Department.

In the summer of my last year there, when my friend asked me to drive with him to visit family members in a small town a couple of hours from St. John's, I was quick to accept his invitation. I never wanted to miss an opportunity to see more of the stark beauty of Newfoundland. I loved seeing its small towns and settlements with their clapboard houses, many of them painted in bright colors, dotting the island's rocky coast.

When we arrived at our destination, he parked in front of the regional hospital.

"My cousin's here. I didn't tell you that."

"All right, but why's he here?"

"He has diabetes. He's going blind, and we're not sure if he'll make it."

Fred appreciated that I told him I felt uncomfortable

going inside, because the two of them would want to talk about their family and other personal matters. I sat on a bench in the warmth of the sun, and alternated between thoughts of the cousin lying ill in the hospital and thoughts of how pleased I was to be living in this fascinating Canadian province. When I noticed my friend walking toward me, I looked at my watch and was surprised that more than a half hour had passed.

"How's your cousin?" I stood up.

"He's in bad shape."

I placed my hand on his shoulder. "Well, I'm happy you got to see him, Fred."

"Thanks. Me, too."

We walked toward the car, and he said he'd like to visit with his other cousins who lived close by. I said I'd be pleased to meet them, so off we went.

The sky had become overcast, and a light rain had begun to fall; the wind off the ocean gave the damp air an unwelcome chill. We drove along the coast for ten minutes or so before Fred pulled off the two-lane blacktop and parked next to a wood and stone, one-story building that looked like a workshop or garage of some kind.

We were walking to the door when he said that the woodworking business was owned by the brothers of the young man in the hospital. After lengthy greetings and bringing Fred up to date with family news, the cousins gave me a quick tour. The shop had the pleasing aroma of wood boards and trim, and clean sawdust that covered the floor. By their placement, the benches, shelves, tables, and assorted tools, clamps, and brackets ensured a proper workflow.

Staining and varnishing took place in a curtained, ventilated corner of the shop. The workmanship was outstanding, and the finish on the coffins was free of defects.

About fifteen minutes later, we left, but not before the three cousins had promised to see each other again soon. I had the feeling they'd be seeing each other sooner than they might wish.

We stepped outside into the damp and chill air, weather that I now experienced as depressing. Fred seemed in good spirits, though more quiet and serious than usual, when we got into the car.

"So your cousin will be buried in a coffin that his relatives might already have made."

"That's right. But it's family."

It was unexpected—but, by now, it shouldn't have been—when he said he hoped I wouldn't mind if we stopped to say hello to his uncle before heading home. Being supportive of my friend, I thought it out of the question to say I wasn't in the mood to visit with anyone, least of all another family member of the young man in the hospital.

"That's fine with me. I'd be pleased to meet him, too."

As we drove back toward town, the clouds began to break up, and the sun once again offered its warmth. I felt better than when we had left the workshop, but that reprieve was short-lived. Fred steered the car into the parking lot of a mortuary.

"Wait a minute. You're kidding me, right?"

He laughed, kind of a chuckle, and said, "Let's go in and say hello. We won't stay long."

His uncle greeted us at the door, delighted to see his nephew and meet one of his friends. The two of them talked for a few minutes about the family and the visit to the hospital. Then, he asked how I liked living in Newfoundland. Encouraged by my answer that I loved living here, he asked if I'd like a tour.

A tour? Who wants a tour of a mortuary? "I'd like that," I said, polite as ever, knowing it would have been an affront to refuse the offer.

The main floor, consisting of lounge areas, was immaculate. Downstairs, the uncle showed me the "prep" room. I had expected to be assaulted by the strong odors of formaldehyde and other chemicals, but the room had a fresh aroma, as if it had just been cleaned. In this second workshop of the day, I learned about the array of tools, stainless steel sinks, an embalming table, and tubes that could have been labeled "OUT," and others "IN." I asked no questions but did a lot of head nodding in response to the uncle's descriptions and explanations.

Both the tour and visit ended about fifteen minutes later. At the front door, I told the uncle that it was a pleasure meeting him and he said the same to me. I had the sudden thought that he avoided what might be a joke within the industry: "You're welcome to come back anytime—dead or alive."

Fred and I walked to the car, but when I touched the handle of the passenger side door, I made no move to open it. "Before I get in, I need to know something. You don't have any other relatives here, do you?"

"No, no. We can head home."

We were the only two people in the parking lot; only one of us was laughing.

On the return trip, at the crest of a hill, Fred pulled to the shoulder and asked if I had a particular denomination of Canadian paper currency. I did, and he said I should look at the reverse side of the bill. On it was an engraving of a wide and shallow valley, the very one now spread out below us, so lovely in the late afternoon sun. We took the road through the valley, and it looked nothing at all like the shadow of death.

GIFTS THAT KEEP ON GIVING

Humor does not diminish the pain—
it makes the space around it get bigger.
—Allen Klein

Beryle and I belonged to that generation referred to as "The Cousins," four boys and four girls, children of three siblings who rest in graves next to each other in a synagogue cemetery in our hometown of St. Louis.

During our childhood, she and I had formed a close bond that remained intact even as our adult lives took different paths, including geographical ones. She never married, but had a large and diverse "second family" in Houston, her adopted home for all of her adult life. Even when social media had become popular and email was in widespread use, we stayed in touch mainly by long-distance phone calls (often over landlines), but no video chatting or anything like it. The many family gatherings in St. Louis were what provided us with the best opportunities to keep up with each other's life. At those gatherings, we would sit next to each other so we could pass judgment on the proceedings and the other participants.

Neither quiet nor shy, Beryle could assume a Don

Corleone style (hereinafter, Donna Corleone) when taking it upon herself to resolve disagreements—such as the one that arose in 2011, when she and I were in our late sixties and one of our aunts had died.

In the living room of the home of the deceased and our surviving uncle, the extended family waited to begin the first evening of *shiva*, the mourning ritual that among less observant Jews lasts fewer than the prescribed seven days, but almost always more than one.

Given the theme of the day, it was reasonable—well, not entirely—that I initiated a conversation with Beryle's only sibling, her older sister Marcia, about two burial plots among a group of a half dozen or more that my mother had purchased in the synagogue cemetery where we had just buried her sister, our aunt. The conversation took only a few minutes to become contentious because of my provocative behavior ("Are you sure about those plots, Marcia?") which, for me, was atypical—well, not entirely. I was casting doubt upon her claim ("Of course I'm sure.") that she had been gifted by my mother the two burial plots that had been gifted to me years earlier—by that same mother, no less, who, at the time of this conversation, had been deceased for ten years, so was unavailable to resolve this dilemma.

As usual, Beryle and I were sitting next to each other. Sensing, as she would have, the exact moment it was required, she shifted a quarter-turn toward me and gave an almost imperceptible nod, accompanied by a *sotto voce* ruling, which wasn't *sotto* enough to keep her sister from hearing, "Your mother gave them to Marcia."

"You're certain about that, Beryley May?" I said. She enjoyed it whenever anyone used the nickname she had acquired soon after becoming a Texan.

"Yes. I am." Another almost imperceptible nod, to accompany another of her concise rulings. "She did."

I wanted even a momentary escape from the crazy conversation; Beryle's Donna Corleone manner provided it by reminding me of something that had happened to my wife's and my friends.

Sam and Patricia make their living building and selling homes. When the buyers, a young couple, decide they want a large deck, but no price increase, our friends say no. The buyers are disappointed, the project stalls—until The Visit. A couple days later, a black sedan with tinted windows pulls into their driveway. The driver, a large, casually-dressed guy, gets out and opens the front passenger door. A guy in a snazzy suit gets out and looks around to get the lay of the land, and waits until Sam comes outside. The ensuing conversation is one of those guy-to-guy things. "So, Sam . . . what's the problem?" He doesn't smile, but doesn't appear angry. Sam figures his only option is tell the truth and hope for the best. "We can't afford to include the deck. It would eat up our profit." The well-dressed guy shrugs his shoulders a bit and says in the same tone my cousin Beryle just used with me, "Sam . . . it's for my daughter. Give 'em the deck." Sam's one-word response demonstrates if not perfect business sense, then at least profound wisdom: "Okaytheycanhavethedeck."

Back at the *shiva*, after my brief time travel, I was aware
that this wasn't the first time Marcia and I had engaged in
the same banter; she enjoyed it as much as I did, even this
time, only an hour after we'd buried a dear relative.

I decided it was a good idea to change the tone—well,
not entirely—of the conversation among my two cousins
and me. "Don't worry. I just like to drive you crazy. I know
my mother gave you the plots, and I'm happy you have
them—just in case you ever need them. I'm happy she gave
you one, too, Beryle, and I hope you won't need it for many
years." That phrasing struck me as comical. "I mean I hope
it's many years *before* you need it."

The truth is, I never wanted the plots; my mother knew
why, and so did both of my cousins. They were well aware
of the synagogue policy that a non-Jew may not be buried in
the cemetery, even if the non-Jew were the spouse of a Jew.
Since that was the case with my wife and me, we'll just have
to wind up elsewhere. And together. As much as I believed
I'd never be buried in the synagogue cemetery, it bothered
me when several times my mother asked, "Have you decided
whether I should give them to Marcia?" I guess it's possible
that I'm wrong about this, but she seemed more concerned
about where Marcia and her husband would be buried than
she was about where Catherine and I would be.

The last time my mother asked, I finally made it clear
that any further discussion of any kind about anything
having to do with cemeteries would be the death of me.
Demonstrating the same sort of wisdom that Sam had
demonstrated during The Visit, I terminated the topic:
"Okayshecanhavethegoddamnplots."

While my cousins and I sat together bantering about who owned the burial plots, we wouldn't have imagined that five years later, after a long and courageous battle with cancer, Beryle would make use of my mother's gift to her. Following an uncommonly beautiful service in the funeral home chapel, I helped bear my cousin to her grave among the many members of two earlier generations of extended family, all buried only a few steps from each other.

Seeing those family graves, I couldn't help thinking about another reason I had returned my mother's gift. When she bought so much of the cemetery real estate, it was as if she had in mind to create something like a postmortem cul-de-sac in a peaceful subdivision. This would have made it much easier for all of the dearly departed to attend a Sabbath or other holiday dinner. After all, no one would have to drive.

Knowing Beryley May as I did, I'm sure she'd agree with me that there's a bright side to her otherwise very sad death. She absolutely loved participating in those long family dinners. She loved to take a position at the table that allowed her to see and hear everything happening around her, and to comment, interpret, and, when needed, rule. Who knows— she and my mother might be busy making dinner plans, including seating arrangements, for the day the rest of the souls of the now-living members of the extended family will arrive—provided they have plots, that is.

It's okay with me that I won't be on the invitation list. I'll be eating elsewhere, but I suppose we can figure out how to

FaceTime or something. The thing is, I'm at peace with the resolution. I always thought each of those extended family dinners had lasted way too long, and I surely didn't want to participate in one that could last forever.

THE LAST FOOTBALL GAME

"Okay, we got one chance only," our coach says. On the grade school asphalt playground, there's no time clock, but a decree from our coach and theirs is just as certain: The game will end after the next play. The school bus has to take us, the visitors, home. The score is tied. We are on offense. If we score, we win. In these seventh-grade contests, the coaches walk onto the playing field to help their teams call plays, and then they stand on the sidelines where they belong. In the huddle, Mr. Dale reminds us—as if we don't already know—we are in a life-and-death struggle.

All of us assume the play will begin with the ball in Aaron's hands, as it has been every play of the game. "We're going to run the Desperation Play." Mr. Dale, a navy combat veteran, recognizes a desperate strait when he sees one. "Myles, line up left. Aaron, throw all the way to the end line. Myles, catch it. Let's go home." With seventh-grade teams locked in combat, there is no time for wasted words.

I run as fast as I can, and Aaron passes the football with a perfect spiral. Over my right shoulder, I watch the arc of the ball as it floats down and settles on the fingers of my outstretched hands. I pull the ball to my chest just as I slam into the chain-link fence.

We win, they lose, we go home on the bus.

One year before the memorable pass and catch, I was ten and about to begin the sixth grade. My family had moved to the new neighborhood, the one with the wonderful playground, a place where kids are meant to have fun. It also was a place where I knew no one, having just left the Rabbi H. F. Epstein Hebrew Academy.

In that quick, intense way kids often do, Aaron and I became "best friends." He was a year older than I was, and at least a number of months older than the rest of the kids in our class. Such were the vagaries of school district age and admission rules. He and I did the kinds of things that best friends do, and we did them well. We both wore the same size shoes, so we'd wear each other's just for fun. If either of us ever needed money when we were together, we'd share whatever we had.

Sometimes on summer nights, we walked to the school playground, which was across a quiet, residential street from Aaron's house, and lay on the asphalt, hands locked for pillows under our heads, lost in the countless stars. We tried to comprehend their staggering number, what is infinity, God and Not God, and what our lives would be like when we were older.

While we lay there on one of those star-filled nights, Aaron said, "Do you know who I'm thinking about?"

"David Medgars," I said, without hesitation, referring to a classmate.

Aaron's "Whaaaaat?" rebounded off the brick wall of the

school building. He sat upright. "How could you possibly know that?"

"I dunno."

To accompany the Desperation Pass, that night, under the stars and on the asphalt, was born the story of David Medgars. Both events were destined to be used throughout the decades of our friendship: "Guess who I saw yesterday?" had only one answer. Our initial reaction to many of life's troublesome developments became "Time for the Desperation Pass."

Another of our most lasting memories was an incident that occurred as we were about to leave for school camp, where each year the sixth and seventh graders spent a week learning about nature, and bonding in the process. To make sure that happened, the teachers who chaperoned us would build bonfires at night, so we kids could stand around together and bond. That was nice enough, but it was not the kind of bonding some of the other boys and I had in mind, and—we hoped—some of the girls, too.

The morning we left for camp, I stopped at Aaron's house so we could walk together across the playground to the bus in front of the school. His mother was determined that he have a handkerchief in his pocket, but Aaron refused each of the three times she insisted. We headed across the playground and were only within shouting distance of his home when we heard his mother call his name. "Aaron. I told you—you must have a handkerchief, Aaron."

We kept walking and kept laughing. Aaron spent a week at the camp with no handkerchief, and we had a great story to complete our trinity of legends: Desperation, Medgars, and

Handkerchief. Since then, whenever we planned an outing of any kind, I'd tell Aaron he must have a handkerchief. He'd say, "I know," and we'd both laugh.

The last time we did this, we were in our mid-forties.

Aaron and I were interested in how other people in our larger city lived. One of the pacts we made in the eighth grade was to take a city bus to downtown St. Louis and get off at the square where a large number of homeless men would sit on benches before leaving at night for the Salvation Army, other shelters, or somewhere in a dark street or alley. We wanted to sit with them and learn why they were there and where they came from. We never took that bus, though we often said, "You know, we really ought to go sit on the benches and talk with those guys."

Years later, Aaron would learn much more about how they lived than we had imagined when we were young boys.

Another decision we made, this time on a Saturday when we were in the ninth grade, was nothing unusual to us, except that we did it: We attended the next morning's Easter sunrise service at the outdoor municipal opera that seated more than ten thousand people. Our Easter adventure had to be clandestine. The plan was for me to be at Aaron's house early enough for us to walk to the service and arrive before sunrise. He was to sneak out of the house before his parents awoke, because he assumed they wouldn't be pleased if he attended an Easter sunrise service, or an Easter service at any other time of the day, for that matter. My parents would have driven us there, but what fun would that have been?

He was waiting outside, and we walked the couple of miles to the opera. It was already crowded when we arrived, but we managed to find two open seats—not in one of the wings, not in back, but almost in the center of the amphitheater. The next morning, the newspaper article about the sunrise service included a large photo of the crowd. To the best of our knowledge, Aaron's parents didn't pick us out among the thousands in attendance; the faces in the photograph were so small and the crowd so large, that without the benefit of an illuminated magnifying glass, it would have been next to impossible to recognize us. But, there we were, Aaron and I, enjoying a lovely Easter morning in the park. We joked that at least the photograph didn't have a caption and superimposed arrow: "Two Clayton, Missouri, Jews attend Easter Sunrise Services."

Judaism was important in Aaron's family. When we were about sixteen years old, he brought me to the orthodox synagogue where his family worshipped. The synagogue occupied a small storefront, operated on a small budget, and maintained separate seating sections for men and women.

In turn, I took him to where my family worshipped in a modern building with a large sanctuary, many meeting rooms and offices, a hallway of classrooms, and a budget that would have supported scores of storefront synagogues. As our rabbi's sermon ended, the several hundred congregants followed our custom and refrained from applauding— except for Aaron. We were sitting with my grandparents, front and center, with nowhere to hide other than sliding down in our seats as far as possible without falling onto the floor. My grandparents looked like they wished we had fallen through the floor, not just onto it.

It's hard for me to believe I'm remembering this

correctly, but about a year later, on another hot and humid St. Louis summer day, Aaron came home from playing baseball and took a drink from the opaque, plastic, ice-water pitcher his mother always kept in the refrigerator. This time, however, he had grabbed the wrong pitcher and swallowed a mouthful of rendered chicken fat, *schmaltz*, his mother used for cooking. He threw up.

The next time he visited the refrigerator and regretted it, he didn't throw up, but did have a major stomachache after eating a few large water chestnuts his mother had placed in a bowl. The only problem was that the water chestnuts were flower bulbs.

These and other incidents convey much about Aaron's exuberance and his admirable ability to immerse himself in whatever he was doing at the moment, attributes that contributed to his endearing personality. It would take time, but these same attributes would acquire a different quality altogether. This occurred first in increments subtle enough that only those close to him might have recognized something was wrong. Eventually, the subtleties would give way to troubling behaviors and thoughts impossible to ignore.

Following our 1960 high school graduation, Aaron attended college in St. Louis, and I left to do the same in Colorado. After two years, he transferred to The Ohio State University where he pursued a program of social studies and education within the College of Education. I saved some of the letters he wrote in 1962, before he arrived in Columbus and during the first year he was there. The letters are intense, and reveal an Aaron trying to find the right path for himself—as all of us were trying to do—in a larger and more complex world than our comparatively sheltered St. Louis community.

I've reread these letters many times. It becomes more evident upon each reading that this is when the trouble was beginning to develop in earnest, though it might have emerged unnoticed or unidentified much earlier.

Columbus, Ohio
Tuesday, August 7, 1962

Dear Hops,
. . . Many odd things have happened to me, being on my own. These things have caused me to realize that life and people are not exactly what I thought they were. I think I've made many of the same realizations that you made after leaving Clayton, Mo. I'd really like to talk to you about a lot of things that you've already had 2 years head start on . . . Your pal, Aaron

Columbus, Ohio
13 Oct. 62

Dear Myles,
It is Saturday night, 9:00 P.M., and I am studying for a philosophy test on Kant. I stop

every 45 minutes to read a few pages of "Pride and Prejudice." On my last break I came across something that Austen says which really affected me greatly. She writes, 'Humility is often carelessness of opinion and sometimes an indirect boast.' . . .

I've really done a lot of reading lately. In the last month or so I've read 1) Lord of the Flies 2) To Kill a Mockingbird 3) Kon Tiki 4) Wuthering Heights 5) Catcher in the Rye. I liked them all especially [here, Aaron had drawn a blue ink pen arrow to Catcher in the Rye.] I can't stop thinking about Holden Caulfield. Can you? Friend, Aaron

Columbus, Ohio
28 November, 1962

Dear Myles,
. . . My next vacation is in the spring and I don't want to go home then either so I've decided you and I should spend it together . . . Ohio State is great except for the fact there are so many bigoted, provincial, narrow minded, conservatives living here. Sometimes I feel like the only liberal-conservative around. I've all but made up my mind to go into social work. I hope to go to either Chicago U. or Columbia for graduate school . . .
Your pal, Aaron

When I was on a break from school in 1963, I visited Aaron at The Ohio State University. We talked most of the first night I arrived, and after a few hours of sleep, he took me to his morning education class taught by a dynamic young professor. However, at the cafeteria where we had lunch afterwards, he was agitated.

"'Kids!' Can you believe he called the students we'd be teaching 'kids'?"

"Yeah, I noticed that. Why'd it bother you so much?" His irritation seemed out of proportion to what the professor had said.

"Because he shouldn't call them *kids*. They're *students*."

There would be occasions in the future for me to recall this conversation about "kids," and realize that it might have been more significant than I had imagined at the time.

Just before graduating in 1964, Aaron applied to the Peace Corps and listed me as one of his references. An FBI agent called to interview me as part of the standard investigation to determine if a person is fit to join the Corps. I remember one part of the interview, close to word-for-word, because I had been concerned that it might have sunk my friend's chances:

"Does Aaron have leadership qualities?"
"Yes, absolutely. He and I were co-captains of the football team."
"I see. So he was popular?"
"Everyone liked him. He's a good leader."
"So, he doesn't like being a follower and has to be in charge?"

"That's not what I meant. He can lead *and* follow.
It depends on the situation."
"So, he's indecisive? Is that what you are saying?"

The interview hadn't kept Aaron from being accepted
to the Peace Corps and being placed in a village in what was
then the Somali Republic. On October 4, 1964, one week
after he arrived, he wrote to me on an aerogramme, that
ingenious contraption with its folding flaps that formed
an all-in-one letter and envelope. From folding it and
unfolding it over the years, somehow I lost one of the flaps;
another small section looks like it must have been eaten
by a mouse. The three-quarters of the aerogramme that
remain overflow with Aaron's enthusiasm about being on
an adventure in the early years of the Peace Corps. And he
was becoming the teacher he wanted to be, in a classroom
filled with students he wanted to inspire and who wanted
to be inspired by him.

After his two years in the Peace Corps, he returned
to New York. In retrospect, this likely was the time when
everything began to disconnect, to short-circuit. He decided
to study education rather than social work, and was offered
a teaching position in one of the city's toughest schools. It
wasn't long, though, before he found himself arguing with
his principal over what Aaron perceived as his superior's
unprofessional and detrimental treatment of the students.
During this period of time, he had married, but his wife
exhibited serious psychological problems following a major
automobile accident. Add to this being drafted in the army
to serve during the Vietnam War, and it's easy to see how

my friend's mental health, which already had begun to be tenuous, would begin to deteriorate.

After about three months of being stationed at Fort Leonard Wood, Missouri, he convinced his superiors that he had to be discharged because his wife's psychological condition and other infirmities required full-time attention. His petitioning must have been intense, and his commanding officer must have decided the best thing to do for himself, Aaron, Fort Leonard Wood, and the United States Army, was to grant an honorable discharge. Aaron returned to New York to care for his wife, who had managed to continue working as a social worker in a city social services department.

Around this same time, the transformation that was taking place began to be more apparent in Aaron's overt behavior. Years later, he would tell me that drugs probably played a role in his deterioration. It would be not at all difficult to believe him.

His older sister, with whom I have communicated at intervals over the years, has refreshed my memory and filled in the blanks concerning the long time during which her brother and I hadn't been in touch. She explained that she first became aware of—or paid close attention to—Aaron's mental state when she and her husband had traveled from St. Louis to Connecticut to visit his family. Aaron had driven from New York to spend part of a day with them.

"As my brother was leaving, he said to me, 'On my way to New York, I'll jump off the Brooklyn Bridge.' I asked him, 'Why would you want to do that, Aaron?' He said, 'Because I can end it all.'"

I asked her what she said at that point, and she told me she advised him that instead of jumping off the bridge, he should stop at Bellevue Hospital and check in. That's what he did, and for emphasis told the doctors that he was suicidal. They admitted him for observation and then transferred him to another facility on Long Island. He loved the facility, but, after a week or so, he announced he was well and left. He began wandering around the country, and no one, including his wife, knew where he was. He supported himself by whatever day labor he could find.

After a while, he stopped wandering and went back to St. Louis to take care of his parents' house while they were in Arizona. There was an opening at a local high school, because one of the teachers had to take a leave for a month. Aaron showed up there and said he was available, and they hired him on the spot as the substitute.

The month ended, the teacher and Aaron's parents returned, and he wandered away once again. He landed in Emporia, Kansas, where he became involved with a fundamentalist Christian community, of sorts. There, two important people entered his life: a "woman" and Jesus. With reasoning that is impenetrable to Aaron's sister and me—and to anyone else, with the possible exception of a small group of commune members—he concluded he should be married again, having been divorced from his first wife at some point during the prior couple of years. In some circumstances, this might have been understandable, or even a good idea. The problem in this particular circumstance was that the "woman" was a girl, around fifteen, and should be thought of as a victim of the beliefs of the commune, the laws of the state, and Aaron's demonstrated powers of persuasion. However, for these two fundamentalists—at least one of whom was an adult with mental illness, and the other a woman-child—the decision to marry might have seemed predetermined; that is, it must have seemed to be God's will.

Soon, they were living in St. Louis and caring for a child, the child of a child. A second child was born, and Aaron supported his family by painting houses. They moved across the river to Granite City, Illinois, where they lived in a trailer, the only housing they could afford. Two more children were born, and Aaron continued to support his family by working as a house painter. It was then the late 1970s and early 1980s.

Catherine and I had moved to St. Louis, and I began to see Aaron again when he would arrive at my office unannounced. I always was available to him. During one of our conversations, he told me he had been a Buddhist for a while, but now spoke with fervor about his Christian religion and Jesus, who, he maintained, was his protector. As he talked, it was impossible for me not to remember our Easter sunrise in the park and his orthodox grandfather, deep in study of the *Torah*.

I couldn't determine then, nor can I now, whether Aaron thought he was ill. I also can't determine whether his professed satisfaction with his lifestyle was authentic or if he was a phenomenal actor. One thing not in question, however, was the comfort he gained from his fundamentalist belief that Jesus would look after him.

He didn't ask, but I offered him a job if he wanted to work in some capacity in the business I was involved in, but he declined. He said he wanted to continue his painting job, even though the work could be sporadic. Because he was broke, or close to it, I offered him money a couple of times, which he took. Both of us drew pleasure from these transactions, which were never uncomfortable; they were in keeping with the agreement we had made in the sixth grade—like blood brothers but without cutting ourselves with a knife—that for the rest of our lives, if one of us had money and the other didn't, the one with the money paid. Period. No accounting. Never.

On one of his visits toward the end of the 1980s, he arrived carrying a rolled sheet of flip chart paper. As we always did during these visits, we sat at the round table in my office. He was more intense than usual, seeming excited but not agitated.

"You okay, Aaron?"

"Sure am. I have something important to tell you."

"What's it about?"

"I want you to run for president."

"You do?" I said. "Why would I want to do that, Aaron?"

Eager to show and tell, he unrolled the paper and placed it on the table. "This is the campaign slogan that will elect you." In large blue letters, he had written, *ELECT A JEW IN '92*. "What do you think? You run for president, and I'll be your campaign manager."

"That's it? That's the campaign?" I thought the slogan was funny and clever; but, out of caution, I responded in formal speech mode. "Aaron, I thank you for even thinking

I am qualified. But, I have to tell you that I will not, under any circumstances, run for president. Not in '92, not ever. You have to stop, because it's a crazy idea." I chose to use "crazy," because I thought he needed to be confronted with how unusual his behavior was. Yet, I had a slim hope that this whole happening might be the product of nothing more than Aaron's sense of humor.

Not appearing to have been offended by my refusal to run, or by my word choice, he asked me to reconsider.

That's when I abandoned any hope that he'd been joking. His presentation was the product of one or more of his distorted perceptions of reality, and there was something about it that bordered on alarming. "Do you know what's the most disturbing thing about your proposal?" I leaned back in my chair to create more distance between us. "You remember there once was a Jew who became a strong leader . . . and I don't have to remind you what happened to him."

He seemed pleased that I finally understood his ingenious campaign strategy. "Exactly. You can be Jesus, and I'll be the anti-Christ."

"No thanks, Aaron."

In addition to my immediate concern about his stability and well-being, there was something far more important to me. Catherine hadn't known Aaron before we moved to St. Louis, but welcomed him when he made unannounced visits a number of mornings in a row, each time soon after I had left for work. In the last of these visits, he said to Catherine that he and I had an agreement since we first met that we'd share money when one of us didn't have any. What frightened my wife, and angered me when I learned of it, was when he proposed that our agreement to share could extend beyond money.

What had been unimaginable during all of the years he and I had known each other, now became necessary. And it was heartbreaking for me. Without explanation, in a gentle but firm way that he deserved, I told my friend that he was not to call our home nor to visit there, but I hoped he knew he could visit me in my office any time he wanted. I didn't know how Aaron felt about all of this because his affect was flat, and he seemed just to accept what I had told him.

Catherine and I were confident our decision had been the right one. This was confirmed not long thereafter when Aaron didn't resist his delusional desire to "rescue" an innocent young girl with golden hair, a total stranger in a Ben Franklin store. He was arrested for touching her, but no one would tell me how he did that or the details of what happened immediately after. In what might have been his last visit to my office, Aaron justified his behavior by explaining that his motive had been nothing but altruistic. "She had blonde curls, and the sunlight from a window made them shine, and I knew I had to protect her from the dangers of this world."

As I listened to what he said he had done and to whom, as I observed his overt lack of appreciation of how alarming his behavior had been, I was worried that he would be convicted, worried that he would *not* be convicted, and hopeful that he might receive the help he needed. The case was concluded without an incarceration and, I believe, without any psychotherapy—at least none that produced any observable change in Aaron's behavior. My concern for his well-being was now outweighed by my concern for the well-being of others, especially the little girl with the golden blonde curls who must deal with the aftermath of an unwelcome "rescue," the product of a grown man's delusions.

We talked a few more times, but did not see or hear from each other for the next twenty-two years, during which my family relocated to Milwaukee and Aaron relocated to an alley behind a grocery store after his wife banished him from the trailer.

To a minimal extent, I remained aware of Aaron's existence through the infrequent messages I received from others who, themselves, had brief contacts with him or had heard from his sister. As a practical matter, he and I were out of each other's lives, though I had occasional encounters with mutual friends, former teachers, and coaches who would ask me about him. I'd tell them that he wasn't doing well and we didn't communicate with each other any longer. It felt more than odd to say these things to people who knew how close we had been.

It felt like a betrayal.

One year before our high school's fifty-year class reunion was to take place in 2010, I learned that Aaron had cancer. His sister told me the malignancy had been discovered as an indirect result of another major involvement with the legal system.

A Granite City, Illinois, police officer stopped him for drinking a bottle of beer while driving his pickup truck. After he made a brief appearance in court, the truck was impounded, and his wife decided this was the right time to tell him that he no longer may live in their trailer. He left as requested and found what he thought would be a good place to live, considering his state of mind and what he could afford: an alley behind a small grocery store.

Now, Aaron was homeless, no more than a few miles from the playground where he and his best friend would lie on their backs and get lost in the stars and wonder what their lives would be like when they were older. We never did visit with the homeless men we wanted to learn more about, but now he had a chance to learn firsthand.

While he lived in the alley, someone from the store gave him a jar of grape jelly, but he had to wrestle with the tight lid in order to break the seal. As he did, he heard a loud pop or crack and felt intense pain in his shoulder. Someone took him to the hospital where it was determined that he had bone cancer. He had one surgery, returned to his homeless existence on the streets, had another surgery, and then was admitted to what his sister described to me as "a horrendous nursing home, just awful."

Hearing what his sister had to say, I found it hard to know what was worse—the alley or the nursing home. The nursing home was so appalling, or Aaron's behavior was so difficult, or both, that even the administrators advised his sister to try to have him transferred to the VA hospital. Before a spot could open for him at the VA, it was time for our reunion.

Without telling anyone else, including me, one of our classmates had called and convinced Aaron's sister to bring him to the reunion. They arrived near the end of the weekend event while we were at breakfast on Sunday morning. Our classmate, Dave, who had made the arrangements told us what he had done and then met them outside. When the three of them entered the room, I joined them, but was disheartened by Aaron's appearance. His arm was in a sling, his complexion sallow, and when he smiled, it was obvious that he had lost two lower teeth. At least he was communicative, and his sense of humor was intact.

His sister walked away to talk with some of our other classmates. Dave asked Aaron if he remembered a specific shot that he had made at the last second that won a close basketball game. Not only did he remember the shot, he also remembered that the coach was annoyed because he had instructed him to pass the ball to our star center.

"But what could he say after the shot went in?" Aaron said, laughing.

As I listened to the reminiscence about the basketball game that Aaron won for his team, I experienced something that I thought was long gone: a disturbing feeling of competitiveness.

In that way a person can feel transported far back in time in but a nanosecond, I was in grade school. Of all of us, Aaron was the best athlete. He could sink a jump shot from twenty feet without much effort, while the rest of us didn't shoot the ball as much as throw it from that distance. He could hit a softball over the schoolyard fence, while the rest of us hit balls that never left the outfield if, indeed, they made it that far. He could throw the football farther than the rest of us. He could run fast, too, but not faster than a few others, I not among them.

By the beginning of high school, the gap between

Aaron and me had diminished, but I always knew he was the better athlete. We loved playing together, although it was not without a degree of competition that strained the relationship at times. We were together on the baseball team, he in left field, I at shortstop, though I was sure he would have been better at that position than I was. We were together on the basketball team, but only our freshman year. After that, Aaron far outpaced me: The next year he was on the varsity team while I was on the junior varsity team. That bothered me, but the coach was right. We were co-captains of the high school football team, he at left halfback, I at quarterback. Aaron's technical quarterback skills were, in my opinion, better than mine, but our leadership styles differed. If Aaron disagreed with those decisions of the football and baseball coaches, he never mentioned it to me.

Listening to him and our classmate talk, I hated the thought that I might have allowed those earlier feelings of competitiveness, and fear of being excluded, to stop me from bringing him to this and prior reunions. As much as I believed that wasn't the case, just being reminded that Aaron had been on that basketball team and I had not, brought back long-forgotten feelings, as if no time had gone by.

During all of the years after Aaron and I stopped seeing each other, it would have been easy for me to find him: I could have called his sister. He and I could have been together, along with other of our friends. He could have attended earlier reunions, just as he attended this one. In part, I had rationalized that I was doing him a favor by not contacting him. I would be protecting my old friend, because I knew how strange his behavior could be. Protecting him? From what? From the judgment of his old friends and classmates? Was I protecting *them*? From whom? From Aaron? From strange behavior? They would have interacted with him the way they did at the fiftieth reunion: with sadness, kindness, understanding, and affection.

Did any of our classmates, or former teachers and coaches who sometimes attended the reunions, pass judgment on my own behavior? Some might have. After all, what kind of person abandons his blood brother?

For most of the rest of his hour-long visit, Aaron and I stood together and talked, just the two of us, as we had done thousands of times. It was difficult to see my old friend pale, exhausted, and ill. When he reached toward his shirt pocket and said that he wanted to go outside and have a cigarette, I encouraged him not to, but at the same time understood that it probably wouldn't affect his life expectancy. Nevertheless, I wanted to care for him.

"I wish you wouldn't be smoking, Aaron."

"It doesn't matter."

"I know you're about to say, 'Jesus will take care of me.' Right?"

He smiled at me and said, "Praise the Lord," then he went outside with his sister to have a cigarette.

My time alone with Aaron had felt more forced than comfortable, more awkward than intimate. I sensed—or guessed—it felt the same to him.

After he returned from his cigarette break, he was talking with some other classmates, including his former girlfriend, and I was talking with his sister. She thanked me for remaining so close to her brother, even though she

knew we hadn't seen or spoken to each other in years. It
was as if she wanted, or needed, to believe that I was one of
the people who were instrumental in helping Aaron attend
the reunion. By not objecting to being the recipient of her
gratitude, I felt like a shameful imposter. But, I said nothing
to her about my feelings; it would be unkind, even cruel, to
destroy her illusion in order to assuage my own guilt.

The cumulative effect of the most aberrant aspects of
her brother's behavior had taken its toll on my willingness
to be close to him again. His marriage to someone around
fifteen years old, and his touching the other little girl with
the golden curls, had convinced me that his letter from
Columbus must have been an early sign of terrible things to
come: "I can't stop thinking about Holden Caulfield. Can
you?" I believe he had begun to imagine he could become
the person Holden wished to be: a body who meets the
little bodies comin' through the rye and catches them before
they fall off the cliff. But, he'd forgotten, or had chosen to
ignore, what Holden had to say about all of that while he
was watching his sister ride the carousel in the park.

> . . . I was sort of afraid she'd fall off the goddam
> horse, but I didn't say anything or do anything.
> The thing with kids is, if they want to grab for
> the gold ring, you have to let them do it, and not
> say anything. If they fall off, they fall off, but it's
> bad if you say anything to them.

It's even worse, Aaron my dear friend, if you *do* anything
to them.

Late the following February, four months after the reunion, I learned that he'd been transferred to the Veteran's Administration Hospital in north St. Louis County, and his condition was worsening. But, instead of visiting him right away, I made one excuse after another: It isn't a good time to travel from Milwaukee to St. Louis; he isn't about to die; he might not even know who I am.

"If you're going to go, you have to go *now*," Catherine said. "You'll regret it so much if you don't see Aaron before he dies."

Before going to the airport the next day, I called Barbie, one of our classmates who lived in St. Louis, and asked if she wanted to come with me to visit Aaron. She did, and she also arranged that Aaron's sister would be at the hospital, and would make sure he wouldn't be given any medication that could make him drowsy. As much as possible, she also would help him ahead of time to remember who we are.

The spring ephemerals were beginning to appear everywhere in St. Louis, above the ground and in the stores. On the way to the VA Hospital, I stopped to buy a large bunch of bright yellow daffodils, thinking they'd provide something cheerful and comforting for my friend living in a place that I assumed would be dismal.

As it happened, this wasn't a VA Hospital like others I had seen: This one was worthy of the people living there. The one-level, modern facility was filled with natural light, the linoleum floors were polished to a high shine, and almost every room had a soothing view of the lawns, gardens, and trees. There were none of the odors associated with nursing homes like the horrendous one Aaron had left.

We walked through the ward doors and were greeted by a social worker. Behind her were Aaron and his sister. As promised, she had prepared him for our visit. He was wide awake after his nap, his hair was combed, and he had on clean clothes. I was surprised to see him in a wheelchair, sitting somewhat slumped and looking much older than he had only four months earlier. He also looked confused.

Aaron's sister and Barbie stood back while I walked to Aaron's side and crouched to be at his level. I showed him his bright yellow daffodils and kept my hand on his left arm while telling him who I was. He repeated my name several times, and I could see how hard he was working. I told him someone else was here to see him. I turned my head to look at Barbie, and she knew it was the right time to join us. Aaron stared at her and then surprised us by saying, "Barbie." He smiled, Barbie smiled, his sister and I smiled, and all of us exhaled.

I pushed his wheelchair toward a sunny alcove furnished with comfortable chairs and loveseats. His sister and Barbie walked a few steps behind, being sensitive, once again, to my need to be alone with him. The four of us sat in the sun and talked, sometimes among ourselves, sometimes directly with Aaron, while he alternated between listening and being somewhere else that only he knew.

He couldn't remember many of the things Barbie reminisced about our having done together when we were younger. There were moments when he seemed bemused by our presence. His behavior resembled that of someone with Alzheimer's. During a number of pauses in the conversation, he said to Barbie, "Now tell me again who you are." But every time she said her name, he would remember her.

I told Aaron a number of stories that I hoped would allow him to remember more about our decades-old friendship. He seemed to be delighted to hear the stories and, in fact, remembered the story about our leaving for camp.

"Do you know what your mother yelled?"

He laughed and repeated the legendary, "Aaron, you must have a handkerchief."

For a while, the atmosphere was filled with laughter and more stories, most of which Aaron enjoyed. At these moments, he seemed to know we were there for him. During an interlude when the others were talking, I leaned close to the nurse sitting next to me and asked what we should expect Aaron's remaining life to be like.

She told me his cancer had spread into his brain and that he didn't have long to live. She said that the night before had been hard for him. His despair had been intense, he was in pain, and he had cried while wondering aloud what sense it made for him to keep living.

"I think his question is a reasonable one," I said.

"Yes," she said. "Yes, it is."

All of us saw that he was very tired, and it was time for our visit to come to its end. His sister helped him into his wheelchair, and she and Barbie walked a few steps down the hall so my oldest friend and I could be alone. In that precious moment of silence, I kissed my friend on his forehead and said farewell. He seemed to smile. Neither of us needed to talk.

Aaron died the following day.

~ ~ ~ ~ ~

A recurring dream. A daydream. A game . . . our last . . . our high school's grass field. The clock shows time for one more play. We are behind by one point less than a touchdown.

"Well, here we are again, Aaron," I say in the huddle. "Time for the Desperation Pass. Your turn to catch it." He nods in agreement.

Players move in slow motion. Everything has acquired such a sharpness from the afternoon sunlight of Indian summer, I can see the stitching and lacing of the ball as it leaves my hand. Aaron runs with graceful strides, and I know there isn't a person who will catch him. He looks over his right shoulder and stretches his arms to their limit as the ball ends its long, slow arc and settles onto his fingertips. He crosses the goal line, turns toward me, and smiles.

The clock is 00:00.

AND THEN THERE WERE THREE

August 28, 2014. "Will you write about me when I'm gone? Like you did about Aaron?" Mickey asked near the end of our phone call.

He had read my story. He knew I had traveled to see Aaron and had kissed him on his forehead to say farewell.

"Of course I'll write about you. But it won't have to happen anytime soon, Mickey. You'll be home in a few days, and we can plan my visit to you."

1971. Mickey and I were nearing thirty when we purchased identical, used Volkswagen vans and converted them to campers. After wandering separate paths within North America, I stopped on the Atlantic coast of Newfoundland, and he stopped five thousand miles away, in Lund, on the Pacific coast of British Columbia.

It was there that he met a woman who had stopped her own wandering. Together, they built a cedar and stone home where they lived for sixteen years and became a family with three children. Then, they moved to Los Angeles. During the next twenty years, they pursued various professional opportunities, the children grew into young adults, and

Mickey and his wife divorced. In 2006, he returned, alone, to Lund, the place he loved the most. He had sold his original cedar and stone home and now began to live in various temporary housing on the remaining acres of his property.

After six more years had passed since his return, Mickey began to build a new home he designed to sit on a bluff with a spectacular western view. In an email to me, he wrote, "I'm not going anywhere else, Hops. This is the last house."

2012. He was approaching seventy and content with growing old. By the following year, everything changed. When I think of Mickey's emails from the two-year period from 2012-14, it's like thumbing the pages of a notepad to create a moving picture, images flashing in rapid succession. Some flashes are most prominent.

- Stage 3 Barrett's esophagus. Bought a food processor.
- Esophageal cancer. It hasn't spread.
- Radiation today. First chemo tomorrow. Oncologist expects a cure.
- Split two rounds of firewood. Felt good. Enjoyed the warmth.
- Most likely have bone cancer. Will know more next week.
- $250 on drugs to counteract chemotherapy nausea, vomiting, bleeding eyeballs, toes falling off, damage to my spermatozoa!!!!
- New watercolor to depict my place in an ever-evolving-never-ending Cosmos.

- Completed 12 weeks of chemotherapy. Will do another 3 weeks.
- Esophageal cancer metastasized to computer. It died. Actually, I think it was another condition having to do with Photoshop.
- Oncologist said cancer in bones won't kill me. Said I'll die from another cancer invading a more vital part of me.
- Will pay your flight from Milwaukee to Vancouver $500-600

July 8, 2014. I called him a few days after reading this email about the cost of the flight to Vancouver. We spent a few moments talking about when I might travel to Lund, and then talked in depth about his artwork, something we had done many times for more than sixty years. This time, the canvas of our conversation was his cancer. Though both of us seemed to understand it was terminal, neither of us openly acknowledged it.

While we talked, I thumbed another of those notepads.

- Skilled drawings by a ten-year-old.
- Early watercolor self-portrait, distorted reflection in bell of trumpet.
- Pencil portraits of homeless men.
- Oil painting of women from India begging for money.
- Print of multicolored koi, swimming in shimmering, sunlit water.

The flickering images halted at a watercolor of a rusting 1940s automobile shrouded by branches and vines that would never lose their grip, and looking as if it would be absorbed one day into the earth of the British Columbia rainforest. A foreboding, prophetic painting.

July 16, 2014. His next email. "Imagine the cosmos, and 2 giant galaxies each with the mass of hundreds of millions of suns, caressing each other . . . This might be my last painting. I am anxious to begin, as Time is flying."

Six weeks later, Time, the poet's "winged chariot," carried Mickey to the Powell River Hospital, where and when this story began: "Will you write about me when I'm gone?" and my answer, "Of course I'll write about you. But, it won't have to happen anytime soon."

I had said this even though it was undeniable that his body was shutting down, piece by piece. A scratch on his calf had become infected and wouldn't heal. The surrounding dead and blackened skin had to be ablated more than once. The hint of wheezing I first noticed a few weeks earlier during our phone calls had become labored breathing.

He said, once again, that he wanted me to come there.

"Of course I'll be there. But, I need to ask, have they scanned your lungs?"

"They did yesterday. I'll know the results tomorrow."

Two days later, he was discharged with medication to control the pain from his new combination of cancers: bone and lung.

September 4, 2014. During one of our phone conversations, he said he was in bed all the time and exhausted. "The home health visitors rub lotion on my legs and back and make sure I have plenty of fluids to drink."

"I can do that for you."

"Sure, you can," he said, pleased, as was I, by the notion. "They also bring groceries."

"I'll go to Lund and get everything you want, and if you can't read, I'll read to you."

"That's perfect. I'll really enjoy that. I think I don't have much hair . . . can't see myself, or turn to see behind me . . . ocean and mountains."

He had oriented his home on a bluff with an incomparable view of the rainforest sloping toward the sound and the mountains on the islands to the west. I refrained from the obvious, "Can't they rotate your bed?" and settled for, "Can they hang a mirror or stand it on the floor in front of you? Never mind, Mickey. I'll do the mirror." What a thought. I'll do the mirror. At the end, the vista he so loved would be reduced to a mere reflection of its magnificence. I resolved to turn his bed to face the wide windows.

When I told him I'd call him back that afternoon with my travel plans, I was thinking about how many times I'd said I would be there, and how many times I'd failed. The trip seemed overwhelming. Milwaukee to Vancouver. Two airplanes. And terminals. Commuter flight to Powell River. Taxi to Lund, where the only coastal road heading north terminates. Expires.

The next afternoon, Friday, I called to say I'd be there Monday.

". . . Oh . . . Monday . . . Okay . . ." Mickey said, each word framed by deep inhales.

"I can get there tomorrow, Mickey. I'll call you later with the details."

A friend who is a travel agent began to make the complex reservation. Certain that Mickey's sister was already in Lund or soon would be on her way from Los Angeles, I called her mobile phone in the late afternoon to avoid surprising her by my arrival the next day.

"Are you in Lund?" I asked her.

"I'm going on Sunday. Since he died this afternoon, there's no hurry."

"Died? What do you mean, 'died'?"

"Died. You didn't know?"

It took quite an effort, but I kept from saying something like, "How the hell would I have known? Would your brother have called to tell me he had died?"

"No, I didn't know. Just tell me he wasn't alone." I could barely speak the words.

"Four friends and neighbors held his hands and feet. He was unconscious, but they held him until he stopped breathing."

Then, she said something I hadn't known, didn't want to hear, and won't forget.

"It's excruciatingly painful to have heard from one of his friends that not long before my brother died, he was sitting on the steps of his mobile home, all alone in the dark, weakly calling his beloved Jumper. 'Jumper. Jumper. Come, kitty cat. Jumper.'"

I decided not to travel to Lund. The three children and their mother, along with Mickey's sister, had to resolve some private and contentious estate matters. Besides, Mickey had needed me while he still lived.

Following his death, I failed to keep the promise I had made to write about him. After several weeks of not writing a word, I sat with the members of a small group that met regularly in a church classroom to read aloud and discuss our writing. I listened to a woman in her eighties read about the still painful loss of a precious childhood possession.

As she spoke, I was distracted by the old-fashioned school clock, mindless of what was in the hearts of all of us who sat under it. Each tick of the second hand, each click forward of the minute hand, consumed bit by measurable bit what was left to each of us. When the minute and hour hands met at twelve, the bells of the church began to toll: "Softly and tenderly Jesus is calling, calling for you and for me . . . Come home! Come home! Ye who are weary, come home!"

A half hour later, under a near cloudless sky, the sun was a warm kiss on my forehead. The kiss I hadn't given Mickey. The kiss he knew I had given Aaron the day before his own death. Trees that had been autumnal gold and red and orange were almost bare. I shuffled my feet through dry leaves, as children do, and created a path like the wake of a small boat in still waters. A quick breeze scattered the leaves and covered any sign that a living soul had passed by.

October 4, 2014. Yom Kippur, The Day of Atonement, a day of fasting and asking forgiveness from God and humans for any transgressions . . . including broken promises. This is not a proper day for writing, but I try and fail. I walk into the garden, the weather perfect for transplanting. The first hard frost is approaching, and droplets of fine mist coat the plants, many still green. With my ungloved hands in the cold earth and mulch, I'm visited by a prayer, the one we sang last night at a Yom Kippur service. I don't consider the meaning of the words, but only how they sound in Hebrew and the melody I have heard since birth:

Aleinu leshabeach la'adon hakol, lateit gedulah leyotzeir bereshit . . .

In the garden, I hum and sing that first line of the prayer, over and over. As I conduct this Yom Kippur service for a congregation of one, bells begin to toll from the direction of the church I had sat in only days earlier. It is noon. It is the hymn I had heard when sitting below the ticking school clock.

The Christian hymn and the Jewish prayer intertwine. Each becomes part of the other:

"Softly and tenderly, *Aleinu leshabeach Ladon hakol*, Come home! Come home!"

I work until it's time to clean the spade and the gardener's knife, scarred from years of use, but still straight and strong. I store the tools in the wooden shed, aged to silver gray. In the garage, sandals replace gardening shoes, but I don't disturb the earth clinging to their soles.

Inside the house, I begin to write the only way I can. I talk with my friend.

Today is Yom Kippur, Mickey. I ask your forgiveness for my not being there to read to you, to rub lotion on your back and legs, to bring you food. My hope is that you drifted away in the midst of a dream or, if you were even luckier, the reality of a glorious voyage to what you imagined might be your place in an infinite cosmos, your final work of art.

Though I try, I can't write anything more.

Winter 2019. I've talked with my friend often since that Yom Kippur when I couldn't write. But last spring, I needed to tell him something special, something I knew he'd want to hear, something I had been reluctant to share.

It's good to talk with you again, Mickey. Can you hear me? It's April now. Every spring, I think about how you and I walked through the woods near your first home in Lund, and gathered sorrel and fern to decorate the table for Passover and Easter dinner with your friends and family. This spring, I've been sustained by the love and support of friends and family after Catherine and I learned there's an intruder in my body. Aaron first, then you, and then there were three. So, it's my turn . . . exactly for what, I don't know. But, from everything I've learned, I do know that if anyone writes about me, it won't be anytime soon.

Time. Does that word still have any meaning for you? I remember how much time went by, and I never really answered what I understood was your question, the one I now ask of you. Where are you, dear friend, when I need you here?

PART VI

In Silence, I Listened

I've begun to realize that you can listen to silence and learn from it. It has a quality and a dimension all its own.
—Chaim Potok, The Chosen

IN SILENCE, I LISTENED

The doctor leans close to me, so close that my eyes won't focus on his face or hands. "This looks suspicious," he says, preceded by the ominous sound of "Hmmm." I ask him why, and he explains it could be some form of cancer, "possibly lymphoma." The word makes it hard to talk, but I manage, "Seriously?" and I notice that Catherine is crying, as I soon will be.

Winter 2018. "You have great veins, so this will be easy," the lab technician in her early thirties said as she proceeded to fill the first, second, third, and fourth vials. As she did, she told me her mother had died twelve years ago, and her mother-in-law a few months ago, both of the same cancer, as it happened. I didn't ask, and she didn't tell me which kind.

"Do you find it hard now to work here?" I said.

"Not really. I like it. I'm happy when people come back for one of their regular tests and I can see they're getting better."

People, not patients. Comforting. Not a great deal, but enough for right now.

Rolling down my shirtsleeve and putting on my sweater,

I watched and listened to her talk with a man near our little alcove. He appeared to be in his seventies, as I was on this day—seventy-five to be exact.

"Oh, yes, yes, feeling much better," he said. They smiled at each other as would a grandfather and his favorite granddaughter.

Catherine met me outside the lab, and we began our long walk to the waiting room of the cancer clinic. Each step down the long corridor led us deeper into the frightening world we had entered together two weeks earlier through the door that opened with a doctor's *Hmmm*.

The corridor was lined with floor-to-ceiling windows overlooking a frozen pond where two large geese faced each other, only a few inches apart. They were as still as the stone statuary we thought they were, until one of them moved its head a few inches to the side.

When we arrived at the waiting room, the receptionist in her mid-sixties rose from her chair behind the counter.

"Good morning to both of you. My name is Judy."

Her standing to greet us was a comforting gesture, even though she did hold a clipboard with attached pen and blank forms, which, when completed, would establish my cancer care clinic identity. Handing me the clipboard, she said, "The coffee machine has lots of options. There's even hot chocolate. Just help yourselves. And remember now . . . if you need me for anything at all, I'll be here for you."

I wanted to believe her.

Catherine and I chose two chairs by the wall of windows that continued another fifty feet to the end of the waiting room. Together, we began the task of completing the four pages of detailed forms. I swore, primarily under my breath, at "List All Surgeries" in the half inch of provided space. I could spell "appendectomy," I could spell "lumbar laminectomy, L4-5," I even could spell "knee," but how can anyone possibly remember, I asked aloud, how to spell "~~cartalage~~" "~~cartilege?~~" My smartphone instructed "cartilage," so cartilage it was.

When we finished the papers, I scanned the room filled with people who waited as we did. Six people, who I assumed were two generations of a family engaged in conversation, sat close together in a rough circle of chairs and a loveseat. One man reached to touch the shoulder of the person on his right, or left, or both at once. Had this been a different setting, like a family reunion in a verdant park, I probably would have a memory of their same behavior as a celebration.

Still scanning the room, the lingering vision of the stone-like geese must have influenced my perceptions. I fixated on a tall man, too thin to be healthy, who stood from his chair by pressing hard against its arms to lift his weight and steady himself. As his long body was reaching its full height, I thought of the tall, straight rocks that stand in the surf at the coast of Oregon. Unlike the rocks, the man bent forward at the waist. He wore jeans, a faded red sweatshirt over his shirt, and knit cap to match, and Nike running shoes. I imagined his long, confident strides during fresh-air runs, now reduced to short, tentative steps toward a waiting room reception desk. A disposable, white mask covered the nose and mouth of a very pale face. I was unnerved by my sudden association: He no longer was stone, but powder, like talc or chalk dust.

I looked away from him and into the expanse of the waiting room. Did any of the people sitting here wonder, as I had of them, what Catherine and I were doing there? Which of us was the patient? Were both of us waiting for someone else—a child? If they did have any of these questions, they might have been answered when I headed to the reception desk and handed Judy the clipboard with my new identity pinioned under a spring-loaded, shiny metal clamp.

I knew that she, in turn, would hand the four pages to a nurse or physician's assistant, who would hand them to my oncologist coordinator, whose introduction to "me" would be, "11:00 a.m., Non-Hodgkin's Follicular Lymphoma, Extranodal."

I couldn't identify the feeling that overcame me. At the end of the counter, there were a half dozen, multicolored, hand-knitted hats, each protected by an unsealed plastic bag. With a measure of apprehension, I slid my fingertips through the opening of one of the bags, traced them back and forth a few times over the texture of the acrylic yarn, and was able to identify what I had felt only a moment earlier.

Lost.

But there was something else. Withdrawing my fingers from the plastic bag, I acknowledged the awful word I wished I could repress.

Contagious.

I knew better. But when I looked at patients with their wheelchairs and oxygen tanks and face masks and pale flesh, I had to fight my irrational fear that they, too, might be contagious. Could they be feeling something similar about themselves and about *me*? They might have those feelings about themselves, but surely not about me. I'm not one of them. I'm far from stone-cold. My skin and blood are warm; my lungs inhale and exhale; when I touch the vein at the surface of my right temple, I can feel my pulse and count the beats of my heart. How can this be real? What am I doing here?

And yet . . . I expected to hear at any moment the dreadful sound of thick, metal doors slamming together to seal us in quarantine.

I might never understand why, but this felt like the right moment to walk to the end of the waiting room for a hot chocolate, even though I assumed it would be insipid and too sweet. Passing a row of people sitting against the wall, I was apprehensive that what I regarded as my comparative strength would remind them—as if their wheelchairs and masks and oxygen tanks weren't reminders enough—of their sick and weakened state. *Should I affect an infirmity, a weakness of my own? Would a cough be enough? Should I limp? So long ago it was that I fell out of bed hoping someone would come to comfort me. At least this time I would be pretending to be impaired so I can comfort someone else.*

I didn't do anything other than nod and exchange smiles with a few people. This behavior made me feel healthy—an odd kind of feeling, given where we were.

Standing in front of the coffee and hot chocolate machine, I was absorbed in my several almost humorous attempts to overcome the static electricity that kept the Styrofoam cup attached to my right hand, then my left, instead of staying in its proper place under the little spout. At last, the cup was where it belonged, and I pushed the start button. Hot chocolate flowed down as programmed. It was more enjoyable to try and comprehend these mysterious forces of electromagnetism and gravity than the mysteries of rampant cell division, radiation, and chemotherapy.

The machine hadn't quite finished its work. Its spout was dripping at a measured rate, like a chemotherapy bag, until the last drop hung suspended for my count of three before falling with a "plink" into the cup. After taking one exploratory sip of hot chocolate, I consigned it to the "Used cups and lids here, please" tray, a better place.

Back in my chair by the windows, I closed my eyes and tried to control my breathing; tried to stay centered; tried to accept that this waiting room, this infinitesimal point in all of time and space, was where I needed to be. As happens in situations like these, a line from one poem or another returned. This time, J. Alfred Prufrock lamented, "I have measured out my life with coffee spoons." While it's not quite the same as coffee spoons, I realized I'd already begun to measure out my life with vials of blood.

One by one, they called the patients.

In silence, I listened for my name.

AFTERWORD

One year later, winter 2019.

Catherine and I arrived at the Cancer Center lab for a blood draw prior to my routine follow-up appointment with the oncologist.

There were about a dozen people sitting in the waiting room, but no one was behind the receptionist desk. Another person, who I assumed was a patient, was standing nearby, so I asked him if he knew where the receptionist might have gone. I figured he'd be feeling the same way I was about these lab tests, so I added that it's bad enough to have to be here, but when there's no one at the reception desk, it's even worse.

He was smiling and animated, even ebullient, when he said, "Honestly, I'm feeling so great, nothing can bother me."

"You sure seem like you're feeling great," I said.

"Yeah, it's been a year for me."

"A year?"

"Cancer-free. They told me I'm actually free of the cancer. I feel great!" He cupped his hand and raised it to the side of his neck. "I had a growth this big. Lymphoma. But I did the radiation, and it's gone. I mean *gone*."

He's familiar-looking, but where would I have seen him? Tall, well-built, looks like he goes to the gym, khakis and a sweater, running shoes . . . the running shoes . . . that's it! The tall, thin guy I'd seen in the clinic waiting room a year ago . . . the one who looked like powder . . . the one I thought I'd never see again because he was near death. His shirt collar and mask must have hidden the tumor.

"Yeah, I had radiation, and mine's gone, too. It can come back, but it's treatable." As soon as I said it, I wondered if he had taken my words as an unwelcome, even hostile reminder about the statistics for recurrence. It *was* hostile. Obviously, he knew about the statistics. Was it his ebullience that I resented? I added an honest, "Well, you do look great. I'm happy for you."

The receptionist had arrived, so I excused myself and walked over to the desk. He didn't follow. He must have checked in earlier.

He really does look great. I don't know . . . I might look pretty good myself . . . at least that's what the mirror said . . . the doctors, too.

A CONVERSATION WITH THE AUTHOR

Kim Suhr, Director of Red Oak Writing: How did this collection come about? Did you set out to write a book from the beginning? If not, at what point did you realize that was what you had?

Myles Hopper: When I began writing, I thought of each piece as stand-alone. Because they contain themes that aren't merely about my life, but are more universal, I imagined they would resonate with a wide range of readers. What I didn't imagine, at the outset, was how much the stories would be linked. From critiques in the Red Oak Roundtables, I recognized the strength and importance of the links, and at that point, I began to write in a way that deliberately reinforced them. It didn't take much time after that for me, and others, to begin referring to the collection as "a book."

KS: You didn't publish My Father's Shadow, *your first book, until age seventy-seven. Why is that?*

MH: Well, the shortest answer is that it's the first book I've written. It feels wonderful that a publisher responded so positively to it. I had become the kind of writer I've always wanted to be, rather than the more academic writer I had been in an earlier career. As a type of prologue to one of the stories, "Sweet Blintzes," I include the only two pages of a handwritten story I had begun to write (pencil on paper from a hotel my father had stayed in) when I was eight, but never finished—at least not until this book was published almost seventy years later. "Author interrupted," one might say.

KS: Plenty of would-be writers might give themselves the "out" of being too old to start a new career. What kept you going?

MH: Part of what kept me going is that no one asked, "Since you published your first book at age seventy-seven, does that mean you'll be one hundred fifty-four before we can read the sequel?" I've always kept in mind that Harry Bernstein was ninety-three before he wrote his wonderful autobiographical book—a novel, really—*The Invisible Wall*. And there were, in fact, sequels. I've received honest opinions of my work and most often have been very pleased by the reactions, even the ones that led me to do some major revisions. We tend to understand and accept that all of us, regardless of age, are working on things that we feel need to be written and read, for one reason or another. We don't always like each other's work, but we always appreciate that each of us is *working*. And working hard.

In my professional life, I've never been reluctant to try new things. I've been an academic, a business owner, a consultant to nonprofits, and held other interesting positions. I've never been deterred by whatever age I was.

This time is no different, except that being a writer means I'm finally doing what means the most to me of any work I've ever done. It continues to be gratifying that so many people are supportive and encouraging.

The work of the older writers—by that I mean around my age, or a bit younger, but at least in one's seventies— isn't necessarily *better* than that of younger writers, but it does include thoughts and feelings and writing styles that otherwise might have been inaccessible at an earlier age. In my own case, had I written this book much earlier than I did, most of the stories would've been less nuanced, and some of them would've been angrier, less insightful, less tolerant of people's motivations and actual behaviors, to mention a few things.

KS: Many people shy away from writing about their lives because of the inevitability of conflicting memories among people mentioned or because of the flawed nature of memory. How did you overcome these issues and find the courage to write about your own life without censoring yourself?

MH: In the Preface, I address my reluctance to write certain stories because I knew I'd have to tell the truth, and the truth—at least as I understand it—could be hurtful to others. It's taken me all these years to feel free enough to write about myself and others who were and are important in my life, but that doesn't mean I haven't self-censored. There are many embarrassing things in anyone's life, and I do examine a number of them that are in my own. On the other hand, I've left out many events that certainly would embarrass me, because I think their inclusion wouldn't add anything important to the book. I also left out many events that might be hurtful to others. Also in the Preface, I quote Joan Didion, who writes that authors "are always selling somebody out." I'm sure about the "selling out" part, but I'm not so sure about "always."

Andre Dubus III suggested that if you're tempted to be critical of someone, especially in a way that would be embarrassing or hurtful to her or him, don't include it if you're doing it gratuitously, for instance in retribution, but do include it if it's necessary to the story you believe you have to tell. I've done my best to adhere to this advice.

There are also the related issues of conflated, conflicting, and flawed memories that inevitably present themselves in almost anything written in the broad genre of memoir. This resembles, in many respects, what often happens with eyewitness reports of the same incident. I mean, remember *Rashomon*?

I compared notes with others regarding certain events and characters. In a number of instances, their recollections led me to modify what I'd written. In other instances, we simply disagree. I've reached a point in my life when I'm able to say to those in my own extended family who might disagree with my memory and interpretations, "Well, I guess you'll have to write your *own* book." I certainly understand why many writers have lost much, if not all, of their welcome at family gatherings.

KS: How did you select the title, My Father's Shadow*? You referred to it at least twice, both at very important points in the story.*

MH: I struggled to find the right title, but each choice just didn't seem to convey what I wanted. First, it was *The Color Red*, then it was *Not My Father's Garden*. When the publisher asked if I had any photos of my family, one that I showed her was what you see on the cover of the book. I'm around age seven or eight and lying on the lawn, and a large shadow of another person covers part of my arm. When I said to the publisher, "That's my father's shadow," she said, "And that should be the title of your book." I agreed with her. A discussion of the photo appears in the first story of the book, and it establishes that the boy is a man now, and the shadow is something he'll never forget, but he has moved far beyond it.

KS: Autobiography, memoir, personal essay, creative nonfiction: there are elements of these various forms in the pieces in this collection. From your perspective, which category most accurately captures the intent and feel of the book?

MH: You're right that the collection is memoir, but it's written as creative nonfiction—although I prefer calling it *narrative* nonfiction. In *Keep It Real*, Lee Gutkind makes it pretty simple to understand what the genre really is: it's *not* okay to make something up; it *is* okay to present accurate information in a way that's more interesting to read, more literary. This explains exactly why the genre is what I'm comfortable using to tell the stories I want to tell. They're true *and* they're stories.

KS: Is this why you choose to write in the genre of creative nonfiction, or, if you prefer, narrative nonfiction? Your essays, as many would call them, read a lot like stories, which you said in the Preface was your intent.

MH: As I was writing *My Father's Shadow*, I imagined that I was reading or speaking to a group. I was telling stories. It's a complex issue where this comes from, but it does have a lot to do with performing for an audience, and why that's important to me. As a young man, I enjoyed being a cast member in a number of plays. These days, as a writer, it gives me great pleasure to read my work to audiences. It's something that just "feels right."

KS: It's interesting that you consider yourself as a storyteller, of sorts, yet you don't write fiction. Or have you, and not included those pieces in this collection?

MH: I do understand the reason for the question, but, as I mentioned, I don't think it's necessary to write fiction in order to be a storyteller. But, to answer your actual question: yes, I've written two short stories that aren't included in this collection. I was pleased when one of them was awarded an honorable mention in the fiction category of the Wisconsin Writers Association's Jade Ring Contest. The other is a dark story about a fictional character adept at performing the Heimlich maneuver. The thing is, I've actually performed it four times in four different emergencies. When I told my younger brother about this, his response was, "Remind me never to have dinner with you." That comment was the genesis of the other, not-so-humorous short story.

KS: What writers or other folks or creative works have influenced your writing?

MH: That's difficult to answer succinctly. Among novels and short stories I've read, I'd include your own recent collection of short stories, *Nothing to Lose*. Your often exotic stories are wonderful illustrations, even for nonfiction writers, of how much can be conveyed without having to overwrite it. Jennifer Trethewey's romance novels taught me a lot about using dialogue to move a story forward. She tells terrific stories, and I'm sure that the way she uses dialogue stems, in part, from her experience in theatre.

I'll skip other fiction writers whose works influenced me and focus for a moment on memoir and autobiography. I've learned from the writing of many, including, to name a few, Eric Motley's *Madison Park*, Geoffrey Wolff's *The Duke of Deception*, Andre Dubus III's *Townie*, Elie Wiesel's body of writing concerning his experiences during the Holocaust, Pat Conroy's *My Losing Season*, and Julius Lester's *Lovesong*. Ed Abell's *My Father's Keep* is a memoir that was especially important to me, given it's deep exploration of the father-son relationship, and the sensitive but powerful way it's portrayed. And then there are essays by Joan Didion, Annie Dillard, and others, including the anthology edited by John Hoyland, *Fathers and Sons*, and the essay collection *And These Are the Good Times* by Patricia Ann McNair, a book that I admire for many reasons, not the least of which is its "pull no punches" honesty.

But, the genre that has influenced as much as any other, and in some ways more, is poetry. I like to memorize poems or passages, and they come to mind in appropriate situations. Hopkins's poem that I cite in the Preface is an example. I could say a lot more about this, but what's most important to me is that when I write, I'm conscious of the poems I know, the rhythm of lines, the imagery, the economy of words in communicating often profound thoughts. For instance, I wish I had written what John Donne did in "A Valediction: Forbidding Mourning":

> *Our two souls therefore, which are one,*
> *Though I must go, endure not yet*
> *A breach, but an expansion,*
> *Like gold to aery thinness beat.*

I mean, how much better than *that* can you get?

KS: What do you hope will stay with your readers after they have finished the book?

MH: It's hard for me to convey how much it means to me that an early reader of "The Color Red" said that the themes of forgiveness and healing gave her hope that she could experience the same in her own life. Another reader said that two of the stories, both about the deaths of lifelong friends, helped him understand that deep, abiding friendships are something that, for the most part, had been missing early in his life. I don't in any way imagine that my book will have that kind of effect on all readers, but it did on those two, and it feels terrific to me as a writer.

KS: Do you have a next book in mind? What can readers expect? Have you begun writing it?

MH: There are some stories I've been working on, but I'm not sure what their final form will be. They might remain as narrative nonfiction, or might be fashioned into a short novel that I have in mind.

KS: My last question is what would you say to someone considering writing their first book later in life? What would you advise?

MH: Well, first of all, I'd say be very careful not to wait too much longer! The next thing I'd say is that you do have something to write about that will be important to many readers partly *because* you're an older writer with perspectives and knowledge that come with the passage of time and the amassing of life experience—even a measure of wisdom. And I'd strongly recommend joining a writing group of some kind and opening yourself to receiving help from others—especially from colleagues younger than you—and offering it, in return. But, I guess I'd end by quoting the title of Judy Bridges' book: *Shut Up and Write!* I remind myself quite often that I should follow both parts of what she advises. After all, you can't do one without the other.

ACKNOWLEDGEMENTS

Completing this book would not have been possible without the support of my extraordinary spouse, Catherine. For your insightful comments and editing suggestions, your astonishing patience in dealing with my astonishing impatience, for your confidence in me when my own would wane, I thank you more than I can here express. You are part of every page of this book. Every page of my life.

It has been a privilege to have worked with Shannon Ishizaki, owner and publisher of TEN16 Press, and for *My Father's Shadow* to be included in the introduction of this new imprint. With their well-known and highly regarded professionalism, spirit, and dedication, Shannon and her accomplished staff at TEN16 Press guided the long, collaborative process of transforming the manuscript into a book and making it available to readers. Thank you, Shannon, Lauren Blue (Managing Editor), Kaeley Dunteman (Art Director), and Veronica Davis-Quiroz (Community Relations).

To Kim Suhr, Director of Red Oak Writing, I express my gratitude for the years of her friendship, her guidance, and her comprehensive editing. Working with Kim and participating in Red Oak critique groups and workshops has been of immeasurable benefit and enjoyment. Her expertise is relied upon by dozens of established and aspiring authors alike, and I'm fortunate and proud to be one of them.

I also am grateful to the five fellow authors who contributed their thoughtful and generous comments that appear on the cover or elsewhere in this book. I admire each of them and their writing, both published and in process: Patricia Ann McNair, Jennifer Rupp (writing as Jennifer Trethewey), Kim Suhr, Ed Abell, and Maurice Sterns.

Lisa Rivero, founder and former publisher of Hidden Timber Books, and Christi Craig, current publisher, offered valuable advice about bringing my book to life. I was honored by their inclusion of "Exodus Redux" in *Family Stories from the Attic*, the 2017 anthology they co-edited, and I thank them for their support and friendship.

I thank Judy Bridges, founder of Red Bird Studio writing center, for her words of encouragement regarding my writing. The title of her widely read book, *Shut Up and Write!*, has become for me something of a mantra during those times when it's hard to put pencil to paper, when every distraction seems urgent, and Leonard Cohen and The Grateful Dead fail as muses.

I'm certain I'll awaken one night remembering someone's contribution which I have unintentionally omitted. I hereby apologize. A number of friends and fellow writers engaged with me in lengthy conversations, and also read early drafts of the book, or selected stories. In coffee shops, restaurants, in front of living room fireplaces, at a favorite kitchen table in Chevy Chase, in emails and phone calls, they shared valuable insights and suggestions that have enriched this book. I thank each of them: Marcia Taylor, Susan Hunnicutt, Maury and Merrily Sterns, Deborah Hufford and Evan Jones, Ellen Suhr, Mark Foreman and Beth Eisendrath, Marjorie Pagel, Jonnie Guernsey, Nancy Martin, Julia Gimbel, Aleta Chossek, Ann Greenstein, and several of my earliest of childhood friends: Noah Newmark, Steven Grand-Jean, Peggy Husch Rothschild, and Karen Sorin, long-lost and recently found, who read and critiqued an early draft of the book, and appears in a story written long before our unexpected reunion.

~ ~ ~ ~ ~

There is a singular expression of appreciation that I've reserved for my brothers, Saul and Earl, both of whom, in their separate ways, would have written differently than I have about the characters and events in *My Father's Shadow*. That didn't deter either of them from helping me recall certain pieces of salient information. Although we didn't always agree on each memory of *who, what, when, where, how, why,* or even *if,* neither brother discouraged me in any way from telling my own story, nor burdened me with any concerns he might have harbored with respect to the content of this book or how he might be portrayed in it.

Any errors in this book are mine alone.